D1130755

The Urbana Free Library

To renew: call **217-367-4057**
or go to **urbanafreelibrary.org**
and select **My Account**

His Greatest Speeches

His Greatest Speeches

★ ★ ★

HOW LINCOLN MOVED
THE NATION

DIANA SCHAUB

ST. MARTIN'S PRESS
NEW YORK

First published in the United States by St. Martin's Press, an imprint of
St. Martin's Publishing Group

www.stmartins.com

Library of Congress Cataloging-in-Publication Data

Names: Schaub, Diana, author.
Title: His greatest speeches : how Lincoln moved the nation / Diana Schaub.
Other titles: How Lincoln moved the nation
Description: First edition. | New York : St. Martin's Press, 2021. | Includes bibliographical
    references and index.
Identifiers: LCCN 2021027559 | ISBN 9781250763457 (hardcover) | ISBN
    9781250763464 (ebook)
Subjects: LCSH: Lincoln, Abraham, 1809–1865—Oratory. | Lincoln, Abraham, 1809–1865.
    Gettysburg address. | Lincoln, Abraham, 1809–1865. Second inaugural address. |
    Lincoln, Abraham, 1809–1865. Perpetuation of our political institutions. | Speeches,
    addresses, etc., American—History and criticism.
Classification: LCC E457.2 .S35 2021 | DDC 973.7092—dc23
LC record available at https://lccn.loc.gov/2021027559

Our books may be purchased in bulk for promotional, educational, or business use. Please
contact your local bookseller or the Macmillan Corporate and Premium Sales Department
at 1-800-221-7945, extension 5442, or by email at MacmillanSpecialMarkets@macmillan.com.

First Edition: 2021

10 9 8 7 6 5 4 3 2 1

For Lauren and Jameer

CONTENTS

PREFACE

Abraham Lincoln authored undeniably great speeches. Yet, especially in his presidential addresses, he often downplayed words, stressing instead the need for action. Mere words could not bring forth the "new birth of freedom"—only battlefield victories could do that. As Aristotle told us long ago, the special virtue required of those in political office is prudence or practical wisdom; making the right decision amid the press of events is crucial. Lincoln had that capacity for political judgment. But Aristotle also asserted that politics is inextricably linked to the human faculty of speech. Especially in democratic regimes, political figures rely heavily on the spoken and written word; through persuasion they inspire the action of citizens. Lincoln was attentive to this necessary sequence of logos and praxis, the way in which our saying leads to our doing. At each step of his political career, the actions of Lincoln were preceded and supported by extraordinary speech—speech that by the compelling quality of its grammar, logic, and rhetoric moved the nation.

Think of the most solemn form that words can take: a promise or an oath binding oneself through words to action. The nation's founding charters were solemn speech of that sort. Promises, however, can be broken, and Lincoln believed that was precisely what was happening in his day. He often used speech to expose the sophistic and demagogic misuse of speech by his contemporaries who were—sometimes knowingly, sometimes not—undermining and overturning the founding promise of the nation. Unlike those who trusted in inevitable progress, Lincoln feared that retrogression and digression were just as likely. He observed how the principle of human equality, which had been clearly articulated in the beginning (despite its egregious violation in practice), was being lost to sight, covered over, distorted, repudiated, and forgotten (perhaps because of its too-long-permitted violation). Lincoln's speeches were directed toward recovery of the nation's integrity, re-conjoining word and deed, promise and performance.

My conviction is that Lincoln's greatest speeches matter as intensely today as when first delivered. Although civil war may not be looming, the republic does not stand as sturdily or as undivided as all would hope. To the extent that Americans are confused about, ignorant of, and—whether consciously or not—departing from the timeless principles of self-government, Lincoln's speeches can once again restore the promise of America by reminding us of the promises we have made as democratic citizens.

As markers of the events that shape collective experience, dates are important in the life of a nation. Especially important are the dates associated with revolutions and foundings; invasions, wars, and conquests; discoveries and inventions; plagues and disasters; the births and deaths of significant figures. We have days that will live in infamy and days of national celebration and thanksgiving.

Abraham Lincoln can lay claim to an outsized number of these dates. There are the Lincoln–Douglas debates of 1858, ranked in the same league with the Federalist–Antifederalist contest over the Constitution. There is Lincoln's victory in the election of 1860, which triggered the Civil War—of all our wars the most costly in American lives and most profound in its consequences. In the world-altering year of 1863, Lincoln issued the Emancipation Proclamation and delivered the Gettysburg Address. The year 1865 brought at least four historic events: the passage of the 13th Amendment, Lincoln's Second Inaugural Address, and the victory of the Union, followed quickly by Lincoln's assassination. Seen in retrospect, his deeds, speeches, and death are unequaled in their entwinement with the fate of the nation.

It seems to me significant that Lincoln himself sought to understand the United States through its chronological milestones. On his analysis, three punctuation points stood out: 1787, the date of the writing of the Constitution; 1776, the date of the nation's Declaration of Independence; and 1619, the date of the beginning of slavery on the North American continent. I list them in reverse order because that is the layered sequence through which Lincoln conceptualized the meaning of America over time. His thinking about these landmarks can be traced in three speeches: the Lyceum Address, the Gettysburg Address, and the Second Inaugural. Two of these are his best-known expressions; the other is, for most readers, a much less familiar

performance dating back a quarter-century before his presidency, the work of a second-term Illinois state legislator who
was all of twenty-eight years old.

Each of these speeches is keyed to one of the foundational
dates. Perhaps as befitted a young politician who had taken an
oath to support the U.S. and Illinois constitutions, the Lyceum
Address grounds itself in 1787, the date associated with the
original form of our government and our political institutions,
which have been maintained, Lincoln says, "for more than fifty
years." Worried about growing lawlessness, mob action, and the
breakdown of democracy, Lincoln calls upon citizens to swear a
blood oath "to the support of the Constitution and Laws."

Lincoln's textual horizon shifts fairly dramatically in the
1850s, beginning with his 1852 Eulogy on Henry Clay, which
opens "On the fourth day of July, 1776" and includes an attack
on John C. Calhoun as "the first American, of any note" who,
"for the sake of perpetuating slavery," began "to assail and to
ridicule . . . the declaration that 'all men are created free and
equal.'" As the repudiators of the principle of equality grew in
number and strength, Lincoln set about demonstrating their
error. Throughout that contentious decade, Lincoln not only
appeals to the Declaration but presents interpretations of it in
nearly every major speech. Only by re-adopting the Declaration could the challenge posed by slavery's expansion be met.
Lincoln's decade of reflection on the meaning of the nation's
self-evident truths reaches its culmination in the Gettysburg
Address, whose touchstone is clearly that charter from "four
score and seven years ago." Post-Gettysburg, Lincoln makes no
further statements about the Declaration; his thoughts on the
founding principles had there achieved their final form.

Other dilemmas still loomed, however. Although Lincoln had been addressing slavery as a matter of public policy since 1837, it is the Second Inaugural that deserves to be considered his 1619 address. Lincoln's reference to "the bond-man's two hundred and fifty years of unrequited toil" in the penultimate sentence returns one almost exactly to the date of the arrival of the first slaves on American shores. Acknowledgement of the significance of this date—a date that precedes by more than a century and a half the nation's founding—did not occur for the first time in 2019 as a result of the 1619 Project of the *New York Times*. Historians like William Grimshaw, whom Lincoln read as a youngster, had highlighted both the far-reaching effects of 1619 and its immorality. As we'll see, Lincoln's reasons for re-minding his listeners of 1619 reach well beyond either the facts of history or a desire to assign moral blame. In quest of national amendment, he laid a path through divine reparations to human charity.

My treatment of these three speeches takes the form of a commentary, which is just a fancy way of saying that I am a slow reader. I proceed paragraph by paragraph, sentence by sentence, sometimes pausing long over just a phrase or a word. No one engaged more deeply than Abraham Lincoln with this historico-conceptual constellation of Constitution, Declaration, and American Slavery; I trust that patiently following along with him will yield fresh resources for thinking about difficult and contested—maybe increasingly contested—matters of American purpose and identity.

A NOTE ON THE TEXTS

The three speeches can be found in the Appendix. My hope is that they will be read before my commentary, during it, and again after for good measure. For ease of reference, the paragraphs of the Lyceum Address have been numbered. Abraham Lincoln often italicized words and sometimes placed entire phrases in block capital letters. This special formatting can be a valuable aid to understanding his meaning. When quoting from Lincoln, I have preserved these features, without indicating each time that the emphasis is in the original. I have used boldface, rather than the usual italics, when I needed to highlight certain words within quotes from Lincoln, again without indicating each time that the emphasis has been added. Similarly, Bible verses, drawn from the King James Version, are given with the original italicization.

His Greatest
Speeches

~ 1 ~

The Lyceum Address

1787 and Reverence for the Constitution and Laws

The Constitution of the United States protects "the right of the people peaceably to assemble." In the wake of the murder of George Floyd by those responsible for public safety, many Americans have been exercising this right. In giving vent to their grievances, a few of those assembling have not been peaceable; the very gear they wear indicates non-peaceable intentions or expectations. Of the freedoms protected by the 1st Amendment (religion, speech, press, assembly, and petition), the right of assembly is the only one to contain an adverbial specification, "peaceably," describing the proper disposition of those engaged in communal expressions of dissent. Peaceableness is a demanding standard—more demanding than non-violence since it applies to the attitude of those gathered, not just their actions. Yet, if being aggrieved and, indeed, outraged is the motive for coming together, then peaceability will be hard, requiring individual and collective self-restraint. The language of the Constitution indicates an awareness of how fine the line is between an assembly of the people and a mob.

The most profound analysis of the dangers of mob rule was offered by Abraham Lincoln in 1838, during another time of national conflict that would, within a quarter-century, eventuate in civil war. Only twenty-eight years old, but already in his second term in the Illinois House of Representatives, Lincoln was invited to deliver a lecture to the Springfield Young Men's Lyceum. The occasion called for political reflection on a fundamental matter, with an expectation to avoid overt partisanship. The theme that the young Whig politician chose was "The Perpetuation of Our Political Institutions."

Presenting a frightening sketch of democratic dysfunction, Lincoln traced a rise in incivility and discord tipping over into political violence and mob action. He showed how the growing lawlessness—and worse, the tolerance for lawlessness—eroded the people's trust in their government. Looking into the future, he predicted that disgust with an ineffectual government would provide an opening for demagogic populists across the political spectrum. Individuals of unbounded ambition would seize upon the disaffection to undermine the constitutional order. From small beginnings in disrespect for the law, the entire experiment in self-government might be overturned.

Having described the disease, Lincoln prescribed the cure: fidelity to the Constitution and laws. Democratic citizenship does not admit of "civil" disobedience. Even unjust laws must be religiously obeyed until they are repealed or reformed through constitutional channels, which include not only election but the broad avenues of persuasion: the rights of free speech, press, peaceable assembly, and petition. This is a cure that is easy to state but not easy to instantiate. The course of antebellum events shows that Lincoln's speech did not bring his generation to worship at the altar of law-abidingness.

If we listen more attentively, perhaps we can do better. With its warning against politically degenerative passions, the Lyceum Address is timeless, speaking to our generation as much as his own. While the basic lines of Lincoln's argument are clear, the details of the speech are complex in their layering and challenging to many of our contemporary prejudices. Our commentary on the text will proceed slowly as we grapple with these difficulties. To prepare, please read through the Lyceum Address, preferably out loud.* Alternatively, you might listen to an audio version, available on YouTube,[1] which will be about the length of a TED Talk.

PERPETUATION

We begin with the title, "The Perpetuation of Our Political Institutions," a phrase drawn from Lincoln's opening paragraph. "Perpetuation" is not just Lincoln's subject but his aim, and as an aim, it might be thought to have a conservative or backward-looking character. The task of the current generation, at least as presented early in the speech, is "only" the task of transmission, passing along our grand and lucky inheritance. Yet, "perpetuation" also breathes hope for the future. Lincoln did not select as his subject "The Decline of Our Political Institutions." That

---

* The full text of the Lyceum Address appears in the Appendix, beginning on page 169. The other two brief speeches are in the Appendix and also reproduced in full near the beginning of their respective chapters.

refrain has become a favorite of grumpy conservatism, from Robert Bork's 1996 *Slouching Towards Gomorrah: Modern Liberalism and American Decline* to Patrick Deneen's 2018 *Why Liberalism Failed*. Lincoln is plenty worried, but the aim of perpetuation is uppermost. He diagnoses the disease with a view to supplying the remedy. Still, he didn't choose a more progressive formulation, like "The Improvement of Our Political Institutions." The Whig standard-bearer Daniel Webster had blazed that path in the peroration of his well-known Bunker Hill speech of 1825. Having praised the founding generation to the skies, Webster confidently declared that the "*Principle* of Free Governments adheres to the American soil. It is bedded in it; immovable as its mountains." Confronting the dilemma of what exactly was left for the sons to do, Webster said:

> We can win no laurels in a war for Independence. Earlier and worthier hands have gathered them all. Nor are there places for us by the side of Solon, and Alfred, and other founders of states. Our fathers have filled them. But there remains to us a great duty of defence and preservation; and there is opened to us, also, a noble pursuit, to which the spirit of the times strongly invites us. Our proper business is improvement. Let our age be the age of improvement. . . . Let us develop the resources of our land, call forth its powers, build up its institutions, promote all its great interests, and see whether we also, in our day and generation, may not perform something worthy to be remembered.[2]

In the Lyceum Address, Lincoln sounds the same note of generational obligation. However, he does not take the easy route of material development, relying on a progressive "spirit of the times" to ensure that the epigones are kept busy. For Lincoln, time has a more grim and foreboding aspect. As a Whig, Lincoln certainly supported his party's policy of "internal improvements" (what we today call "infrastructure"). Yet, in the Lyceum Address he makes no mention of it; or rather, he gives it a startling and spiritualizing twist. His version of internal improvements applies directly to the substrate of the individual soul. The only use of the word "improve" comes in the penultimate paragraph, where it refers not to the building of bridges and canals but to the mining of the "solid quarry of sober reason" in order to fashion "other pillars" for "the temple of liberty." Lincoln's peroration is more foundational and audacious than Webster's.

Assuming Lincoln chose his words carefully, it's worth noting that "perpetuation" has a different valence than either "conservation" or "preservation," both of which are rooted in keeping and guarding (the Latin *servare*). They describe defensive acts. And if we remember their household meaning—the putting up of preserves and conserves—they involve altering the original (by canning and pickling) as a hedge against future need. By contrast, the entire focus of "perpetuation" is on the everlasting, the eternal, the unchanging. To perpetuate is to cause to endure indefinitely. However, the word by itself does not indicate the means (old modes or new) by which to achieve that result. Lincoln's subject of perpetuation requires an inquiry into the nature of time and causation. It hints at metaphysical as well as political questions.

Unlike "conservation" or "preservation," Lincoln's choice of "perpetuation" has religious resonance. That note is heard, with trumpet clarity, in the very last line of the address, when Lincoln compares our political institutions to "the only greater institution"—the Church—so rock-solid in its foundations that "the gates of hell shall not prevail against it." The Bible reference is to Matthew 16:18, where Jesus founds his Church on Peter's faith in the revealed Messiah. Could a political founding rival that? Is there a death-proof form of government? Lincoln does declare in paragraph 4 that "As a nation of freemen, we must live through all time, or die by suicide." This question of whether free government can endure—and what is necessary to make it endure—preoccupied Lincoln from the beginning.

Lincoln will return to this word "perpetuation" with a vengeance in his contest with Stephen Douglas, beginning with the Peoria Address in 1854 and peaking in the Lincoln–Douglas debates of 1858. There he sets the perpetuation of free institutions, premised on the principle of human equality, in direct opposition to the perpetuation of slavery. The sure consequence of allowing slavery to spread throughout the territories would be its perpetuation. Not by accident did the most radical supporters of slavery become known as the "Perpetualists."[3] Lincoln countered that the perpetuity of the Union could be secured only by placing slavery back where the founders had originally placed it, namely, "in the course of ultimate extinction" (a phrase he employed dozens of times in his campaign speeches of 1858). Understood as a transient evil, the institution of slavery could be temporized with (to a degree), but if ever it became "perpetual and national," it would mean that the gates of hell had prevailed.[4]

By their nature, political communities aim to endure. Rome is not uniquely "the eternal city." As Lincoln would assert in his

First Inaugural, "Perpetuity is implied, if not expressed, in the fundamental law of all national governments." Even the earlier and less "national" of our national charters, the Articles of Confederation, bore as their full title, "Articles of Confederation and Perpetual Union." The first object of the Constitution is the formation of "a more perfect Union," one more likely to be perpetual because less prone to disintegration.

GEORGE WASHINGTON AND
OUR POLITICAL INSTITUTIONS

Having explored some of the connotations of "perpetuation," what can be said about the rest of the title: "our political institutions"? Nowhere does Lincoln define this term, although he does on second reference call it "a system of political institutions." Moreover, when he initially spells out the "something of ill-omen amongst us," what he describes is how mob rule displaces each of the three branches of government. There is "increasing disregard for law" (the legislative function); there is a "growing disposition to substitute the wild and furious passions, in lieu of the sober judgment of Courts" (the judicial function); and finally, "the worse than savage mobs" replace "the executive ministers of justice" (the executive or police function). Although the phenomenon he describes goes by the name "mob law," strictly speaking the mob is lawless and despotic. It fits the very definition of arbitrary rule: unlimited, unrestrained, capricious. By contrast, these constitutionally articulated parts divide and check power through their complex relation to one another. They are what Lincoln means by "our political institutions."

The modifier that Lincoln more frequently attaches to the

word "institutions" is "free." In his first appearance on the political stage, announcing his candidacy for office in 1832, Lincoln endorsed public education so that citizens might, through
the reading of history, "duly appreciate the value of our free
institutions." He makes a similar linkage here, telling us that
the system of political institutions serves "the ends of civil and
religious liberty" and that the whole elaborate arrangement requires "general intelligence" on the part of the people. Interestingly, Lincoln rapidly shifts from the flat and nearly always
boring word "institutions" to something more tangible—"the
fabric of freedom"—and architectural—"a political edifice of
liberty and equal rights" and a "temple of liberty" supported by
"props" and "pillars." Along with enlivening the subject, these
images imply that means and ends are inseparably joined into
one structure. Of course, this manner of speaking is not Lincoln's invention; these are well-worn republican tropes.

George Washington in his Farewell Address had deployed
many of these same metaphors while highlighting his concern
for the nation's institutions. The verbal echoes between Washington's last address and Lincoln's first are numerous, suggesting
that the primary text to which the Lyceum Address is beholden
is that most famous speech of warning from 1796. Washington
celebrates Union as "a main Pillar in the Edifice of your real
independence," and "a main prop of your liberty." Lincoln, too,
sees "props" and "pillars," but in examining the materials out
of which they are formed, he finds some to be "decayed, and
crumbled away." Washington warns against sectionalism that
would "tend to render Alien to each other those who ought to
be bound together by fraternal affection"; Lincoln worries about
"the alienation of their affections from the Government"—a

generalized, rather than sectional, alienation felt by "the American People."[5] Washington announces in the strongest terms that compliance with the law and the Constitution is "sacredly obligatory upon all"; the lesson in democratic theory is reiterated by Lincoln and supplemented with his call for a "political religion" of "reverence" for the Constitution and laws. Washington inveighs against the dangerous effects of "the strongest passions" and the "cunning, ambitious and unprincipled men" who would "usurp for themselves the reins of Government"; Lincoln, too, disparages passion—calls it "our enemy"—and puts us on guard against the unbounded ambition of the republic-destroyers.

Despite his clear debt to Washington (and Washington's dynamic speechwriting duo, Hamilton and Madison), Lincoln did not just present a warmed-over version of the Farewell Address. Nonetheless, his route to originality was through the fullest possible assimilation of his borrowed sources, thinking through and then beyond them. Lincoln achieves this internalized appropriation with many authors who were dear to him. So, for instance, while erudite preachers and public men could high-tone their rhetoric with a spot-on quote or two from Shakespeare, Lincoln did something quite different. He rarely quoted or made any direct application of his sources; instead, he made the insights and phraseology his own to such an extent that he could refigure and transpose them, like a musician whose innumerable borrowings and variations are bodied forth in new and unexpected forms. Through the compressive power of his mind, Lincoln metamorphizes his sources.[6]

By many measures, Washington's is the more comprehensive of the two addresses. He discusses matters that Lincoln does not, such as sound fiscal practices and prescriptions for good administration. He devotes considerable attention to matters that Lincoln mentions dismissively, such as threats from abroad. Lincoln's unconcern about foreign interference—"Shall we expect some transatlantic military giant, to step the Ocean, and crush us at a blow? Never!"—is probably the most noticeable difference between the two addresses. Although they share an interest in the health of institutions, for Washington this includes fears about the possible skewing of the separation of powers; thus, he warns against "the spirit of encroachment" on the part of officeholders and the danger of "change by usurpation." (This incremental erosion of limited government is today justified under the fetching name of "the living Constitution.") Although Lincoln will also employ the word "usurpation," he frames it quite differently—extra-constitutionally, we might say.

While his reflections encompass the whole political scene, Washington is most concerned with the character of the citizenry, which he regards as the precondition for the maintenance of free institutions. As Lincoln put it in the debate at Ottawa, having learned it from Washington:

> In this and like communities, public sentiment is everything. With public sentiment, nothing can fail; without it nothing can succeed. Consequently he who moulds public sentiment, goes deeper than he who enacts statutes or pronounces decisions. He makes statutes and decisions possible or impossible to be executed.

In the Farewell Address, Washington is engaged in this ultimate task: shaping a fundamental and enduring public sentiment that will shore up—and just as importantly, frame (by restricting or

keeping within bounds)—the efforts of future American statesmen. Hence Washington's unabashed appeal to "religion and
morality" as the "indispensable supports" of "political prosperity," the "great Pillars of human happiness," and the "firmest
props" of citizen duty. While political institutions are distinct
from the institutions of civil society (families, schools, and
churches), Washington believes these two sets of institutions are
profoundly interdependent. Lincoln also summons these other
institutions (starting with "every American mother") to come
to the aid of our political institutions by inculcating "the political religion" of law-abidingness. Neither statesman subscribes
to the view that political institutions alone can produce the required republican mores. In this, they dissent from the modern
(or Enlightenment) confidence that public benefits can reliably
flow from the clever channeling of private vices. They would
not have joined in the optimistic prediction made by Immanuel
Kant in "Perpetual Peace": "The problem of organizing a state,
however hard it may seem, can be solved even for a race of dev-
ils, if only they are intelligent." While not scorning the ingenious mechanics of "the new science of politics"—summed up
in Federalist 51's motto: "ambition must be made to counteract
ambition"—Washington and Lincoln keep foremost a concern
for character, morality, and virtue. It is on this score especially
that Lincoln's address is the more profound one. Like a river
through a narrow canyon, the Lyceum Address cuts deeper in its
analysis of the passions of both the few and the many, deeper in
its grappling with the human temptation to tyranny, deeper in
its portrait of the mob and its motives, deeper in its understanding of public opinion, and, consequently, deeper in its rhetorical
presentation.[7]

THE DOUBLENESS OF TIME

Having forthrightly stated his topic, Lincoln devotes a substantial paragraph to describing the enviable heritage of the post-founding generations. He begins: "In the great journal of things happening under the sun, we, the American People, find our account running, under date of the nineteenth century of the Christian era." Don't be too quick to dismiss this as the kind of boilerplate typical of an immature writer living in an age that favored the florid. I submit that anyone who can compose such a sentence is engaged in serious reflection on the human situation and its horizoning. Lincoln adopts a dual perspective. There is the order of nature, "under the sun," and there is a human calendar, an agreed-upon measurement of time that sets us in the nineteenth century. There is Nature and there is Convention. However, it's more complicated than that, since the Gregorian calendar begins from a world-historical event, the birth of Jesus, that marks—or is understood by believers to mark—the most dramatic entry of God into human history. This great diremption divides time into B.C. (before Christ) and A.D. (*anno Domini*, in the year of our Lord). We live under the sun and under the Son—Nature and Revelation. Even those who today wish to remain neutral with respect to the truth of that event by adopting B.C.E. (before the common era) and C.E. (the common era) are still acknowledging its trans-political, epoch-making significance. Moreover, if what the date marks is true, then God is superior to the order of nature, acting at will in contravention of that order. Lincoln's presentation suggests questions—centering on how nature, convention, and revelation are related—but does not resolve them.

Lincoln's sentence echoes the opening clause of the Declaration, "When in the course of human events," as well as the opening clause of the Constitution, "We the People," except that the human event that formed the "American People" is situated by Lincoln within two wider realms: cosmic nature and Christianity. While the Declaration included a reference to the "laws of Nature and Nature's God" (deistic at best), along with references to a creating and providential God (monotheistic but not specifically Christian), Lincoln does not elide or subsume the tension between physics and metaphysics in a bland, generalized theism. If anything, he doubles down on the dualism. Thus, a few lines further on, he invokes "fate." We are encouraged to carry out our task of perpetuation "to the latest generation that fate shall permit the world to know." Why fate? Why not the Almighty? What will determine the end of the world? Will it be an ineluctable chain of cause and effect, the entropy of the second law of thermodynamics, or the return of Christ in power and glory? In the peroration of the Lyceum Address, Lincoln will circle back to the end times, but for now, he starts us off with hints and flashes.

THE AMERICAN ACCOUNT

Another unusual feature of Lincoln's scene-setting is the presentation of the world as a kind of text, like a ledger or almanac. Whereas the Declaration of Independence described human events as having a "course," like the flow of a river, thus assimilating political history to nature, Lincoln nearly reverses this. He speaks of an American "account" within "the great journal of things happening." It is as if his intense bookishness turns all things into documents that can be read. Accommodating the passage of time, the American "account" is said to be "running." Now, Lincoln knew a bit about "running accounts" (that is, open, unsettled, revolving credit); his partnership in a general store that went bankrupt in 1833 saddled him with debt that he was still paying down at the time of the Lyceum Address. This is not the only occasion on which Lincoln conceives of the nation itself as a tally sheet of debits and credits. Just as he deploys religion for political effect, he does the same with economic language and concepts. The most profound instance will come in the Second Inaugural, with its vision of a blood price coming due. Post-Lincoln, the best-known example of such appropriation is probably Martin Luther King, Jr.'s "I Have A Dream" speech. Describing "the magnificent words of the Constitution and the Declaration of Independence" as a "promissory note" for every American, King then demands that the nation stop kiting checks.

If the beginning is half of the whole, Lincoln's beginning promises much. He has introduced the twin themes of time (itself double) and text. Both themes will be extensively developed as he revisits, intertwines, and extends their meanings. Only after this complex positioning of his generation does Lincoln survey the situation, informing the Americans of 1838 that they are the "legal inheritors" of two "fundamental blessings": basically, land and liberty. The analysis follows the nature/convention distinction already established. Americans enjoy both a natural environment—"the fairest portion of the earth, as regards extent of territory, fertility of soil, and salubrity of climate"—and a built environment—with a "government" that comes closer to "civil and religious liberty" than any before it. Both legacies must be transmitted to the next generation. As already mentioned, Lincoln foresees no difficulty in passing along "this goodly land . . . unprofaned by the foot of an invader." Serving as a caretaker of the "political edifice," however, is trickier, since the initial threat to it comes from an unavoidable source: time itself. Lincoln says it is our task to transmit the "political edifice . . . undecayed by the lapse of time and untorn by usurpation." The first threat is insidious. As time elapses, we lapse. Almost imperceptibly, institutional decay sets in. The second threat sounds violent. Presumably, usurpation could occur either as the coup de grâce toppling already hollowed-out institutions or, more dramatically, as an assault on a relatively healthy body politic, tearing into it. Both dangers—the chronic one of time and the acute one of usurpation—arise from within. They are forms of suicide, bringing about the self-destruction of self-government.

DOUBLE VISION

Lincoln's penchant for viewing things from different angles, and even from radically reversed perspectives, continues throughout the speech. These doublings and reconsiderations are, in fact, a major structural feature of the address. Among the main ones: Lincoln gives two very different accounts of the founding generation; he gives two very different accounts of the lynchings that occurred in Mississippi and St. Louis; analytically, he divides the effects of mob rule into two categories (direct and indirect); he discerns two types of danger (current and prospective) and, accordingly, offers two different solutions (reverence and reason); finally, he examines the problem of the passions in its different manifestations in the few and the many (those timeless political categories).

The most dramatic of these doublings are his stories of mob rule in action. He tells of two instances—and then retells each one. Calling these instances "revolting to humanity," Lincoln describes how in Mississippi the mobs first targeted gamblers, then proceeded to lynch negroes, "white men, supposed to be leagued with the negroes," and finally visitors from other states. He develops a lurid simile: "dead men were seen literally dangling from the boughs of trees upon every road side; and in numbers almost sufficient, to rival the native Spanish moss of the country, as a drapery of the forest." Not by accident, Lincoln will return to the forest imagery at the very end of the address when he laments the passing of "the forest of giant oaks." The nation's degeneration over time is captured in these twin images, as the majestic oaks (emblem of the revolutionary generation)—now "despoiled," "shorn," and "mutilated"—are replaced by the corpses of the innocent. The whole passage is reminiscent of a lyric written a full century later by Abel Meeropol in 1937, and recorded most famously by the great Billie Holiday: "Black bodies swinging in the southern breeze / Strange fruit hanging from the poplar trees."

Moving to "that horror-striking scene at St. Louis" (again, note the parallel and contrast to "the interesting scenes of the revolution"), Lincoln does all he can to shock his audience into sympathy with the victim: "A mulatto man, by the name of McIntosh, was seized in the street, dragged to the suburbs of the city, chained to a tree, and actually burned to death; and all within a single hour from the time he had been a freeman, attending to his own business, and at peace with the world." After relating these "most highly tragic" tales, Lincoln interrupts himself with a question—a question that he attributes to his audience: "But you are, perhaps, ready to ask, 'What has this to do with the perpetuation of our political institutions?'"

This is a favorite rhetorical technique of Lincoln's. Through the judicious use of questions, he often creates a dialogic engagement with the audience. Sometimes, as here, he puts words directly in the mouth of an objector or naysayer, thus allowing likely grounds of resistance to be expressed and responded to. Other times he poses the questions himself, as a way of advancing the argument and helpfully signaling its new phases. Before this present question, he had already posed five others; and there are seven more that follow.[8] Significantly, however, this is the only one of the thirteen to be ascribed to "you"—his listeners.

Why does Lincoln anticipate push-back at this point? Today, we are properly horrified by the nation's history of lynchings and mob violence. But Lincoln was addressing an audience that might have felt some sympathy with the mob or, at least, sympathy with its motives if not its actions. What were those motives? We might assume "racism," but during these decades, from 1830 to the Civil War, the majority of extrajudicial hangings were actually of whites. Lincoln's examples, however, were not of cattle-rustlers or horse thieves subject to frontier justice. He cites Mississippi, noting that the outbreak of violence there began with opposition to riverboat gamblers. Although gambling had been recently legalized in the state, many citizens, and those perhaps the most upstanding, were morally outraged by the activity. They were angry at the perceived injustice of the gamblers as well as the perceived injustice of the new law allowing gambling. Anger is a potent sign of a thirst for justice, a thirst

powerful enough to send human beings outside the law, especially when the law is slow or unreliable or simply wrong. The
quest for morality and justice (as those concepts were understood by popular sentiment) drove the formation of vigilance
committees in Mississippi and the eventual resort to extrajudicial violence.

During this same time, public opinion was greatly aroused
against the new type of messianic abolitionist who was intem-
perate in speech and intolerant of political compromise. William
Lloyd Garrison's newspaper, *The Liberator*, had been founded in
1831, followed by the establishment in 1833 of the American
Anti-Slavery Society, which called for the immediate and uncon-
ditional end of slavery. Like the gamblers, radical abolitionists
were engaged in a legal but extremely unpopular activity. This
was the height of the abolitionist petition movement, which
provoked the imposition of the "gag rule" in Congress and the
ensuing controversy over whether this violated the people's
constitutional right of petition. Anti-abolitionist furor extended
well beyond the slave states and was strongly felt in Illinois. In
1837, the Illinois legislature joined other free states in passing
resolutions condemning abolitionism. Significantly, out of 101
Illinois legislators, Lincoln was one of only six to vote against
the resolutions. Moreover, he, joined by a lone colleague, took
the further step of filing a formal protest against the Illinois
Anti-Abolition Resolutions.[9]

Adding to the ferment, ever since Nat Turner's rebellion in
Virginia in 1831, fears and rumors of slave revolts abounded. As
noted by Lincoln, these overblown suspicions were the catalyst
for the events in Mississippi. According to a twentieth-century
scholar, "the people of Mississippi were terrified by a pamphlet

published in 1835 . . . purporting to reveal the plot of an extensive slave uprising in the South led by white desperadoes, chief
of whom was John A. Murrell," an infamous highwayman.[10]
The newspapers made matters worse by inciting and then jus-
tifying vigilantism, arguing that the safety of the community
was the supreme law. In the Lyceum Address, Lincoln describes
the frightful result of this popular frenzy. What goes unmen-
tioned (for the moment) is the event closest to home, the murder of abolitionist Elijah Lovejoy. Lovejoy had begun publishing
an anti-slavery newspaper in 1837 in Alton, Illinois, after being
driven out of St. Louis, just across the Mississippi. By November
1837, Lovejoy had been shot in a melee and his printing press
was hurled into the river.

In selecting his examples of mob rule, Lincoln quite deliberately avoids the incident uppermost in the minds of his audience. His purpose, however, is not to defer to the sensitivities of
his audience, but rather, by temporarily avoiding that specific
incident, to induce them to lift their sights to the larger matters
that are at stake and, in fact, to help loosen the hold of their immediate passions so they can reason together.

Lincoln knows how difficult it is to challenge popular passion
directly. Those in the grip of anger—and, worse, anger compounded by fear—are resistant to any appeal to sympathy for
their victims. They want sympathy for themselves. Aware of
this resistance, Lincoln insists on giving it a voice. He models
civil discourse for them. The "you" of his audience does not
come right out and say, "What's the big deal, those thugs deserved what they got." Rather, they say something defensive but
still responsive to the broader topic. They ask, "What has this to
do with the perpetuation of our political institutions?" To prove

that "it has much to do with it," Lincoln first agrees, at least in part, with the objectors. He grants that the gamblers "constitute a portion of population, that is worse than useless in any community." Lincoln imagines a pleasing scenario in which this unwelcome category of persons is "annually swept, from the stage of existence, by the plague." Were nature to produce a morally discriminating virus, "honest men would, perhaps, be much profited, by the operation." In the short space of a few paragraphs, Lincoln has reversed the perspective. We move from a description of the Mississippi hangings as "revolting to humanity" to the thought that these deaths are "never matter of reasonable regret."

This reversal of perspective is even more shocking in the second telling of the "highly tragic" story of the killing of McIntosh. Now we learn he was not just minding his own business; he had committed a heinous murder. Since "he must have died by the sentence of the law," for him "it was as well the way it was." Lincoln vouches that this is "the correct reasoning, in regard to the burning of the negro at St. Louis"—note he is no longer a "mulatto man, by the name of McIntosh," but a "negro" stripped even of his name. This sounds awfully hardhearted. Lincoln first tried an all-out appeal to sympathy for the victims, and then, anticipating the failure of that emotional appeal, shifted to this very stark, callous reconsideration. "Abstractly considered," the direct consequences of mob rule are of "little consequence."

By juxtaposing these two antithetical perspectives (humanitarianism versus morally discriminating calculation), Lincoln is indicating that any approach that focuses only on the direct effects of mob rule is bound to be unproductive, since the wider public (some small part of which is acting as a mob) basically welcomes the outcome: gamblers and murderers quickly dispensed with. Lincoln disposes his audience to listen to him by validating their instinctive hostility to wrongdoers. Two things, however, should be noted: first, he renders their concern with justice less heatedly angry and more coolly calculative; and second, in the retelling of the events in Mississippi, he refers only to the gamblers at Vicksburg, saying nothing about the violence toward allegedly conspiring slaves, their supposed white allies, or suspicious outsiders. By leaving the racially charged and xenophobic lynchings out of his retelling, he says nothing to belittle those deaths or to modify his initial horrifying portrait.

THE CASE FOR THE LAW

Having befriended the vigilantes and their defenders (to the extent his own convictions permit), Lincoln can now shift their attention to consequences—indirect and prospective—that may have escaped their notice.[11] Describing how the contagion of mob violence spreads and assumes more threatening forms, Lincoln begins, as he very often does, near the viewpoint of his listeners. Thus, rather than appealing altruistically to their concern for others, he appeals instead to their self-interest, but in a way that demonstrates the linkage between their self-interest and the cause of law-abidingness.[12] Accordingly, his first point is that the mob might make mistakes and catch up some of its own for summary punishment. Even mobocrats are not safe from mobocracy. From there, he widens the circle of concern to the truly innocent, "those who have ever set their faces against violations of law in every shape." Without using legal language like "due process," this section vindicates the procedural component of justice. Lincoln sticks with his architectural imagery, speaking of "the walls erected for the defence of the persons and property of individuals." Without these protective barriers, one gets an alternative sort of process: the "process of hanging" (from gamblers to negroes to white citizens to strangers) that went on in Mississippi.

Once the rule of law is "trodden down," the consequences are far-reaching. Lincoln's next point is that the vigilantes have released something they did not anticipate. In their impatience, they skirted the law in pursuit of justice (as they understood it). Since popular opinion was in sympathy with their conception of justice, the perpetrators went unpunished. That corruption breeds another corruption: when "the lawless in spirit" see that the vigilantes have free rein, they take that as an invitation "to become lawless in practice." The vigilantes meant to crack down on crime. Lincoln tells them they have emboldened the criminals. When law is disregarded for the sake of justice, that provides license for those who would disregard law for purposes of their own. Lincoln doesn't indicate how many people fall into this category of the "lawless in spirit" who are kept in check only by fear of punishment, but he is emphatic that there are those who regard "Government as their deadliest bane" and who will "make a jubilee of the suspension of its operations." Not only does mob justice always carry this danger, but even some forms of legitimate protest, like those involving mass direct action, can spiral out of control. Civil unrest is always an occasion for opportunistic looters and scammers, the "lawless in spirit" becoming "lawless in practice."

Meanwhile, societal breakdown has a very different effect on good citizens. When government proves ineffectual, the tranquility-loving, law-abiding people lose trust in it. According to Lincoln, "the alienation of their affections from the Government" is the worst effect of the "mobocratic spirit." Political scientists and public intellectuals have tracked rising levels of distrust, cynicism, and apathy among Americans since the turmoil-filled 1960s and '70s, echoing Lincoln's conviction that "the *attachment* of the People" is "the strongest bulwark of any Government, and particularly of those constituted like ours." Democratic government really does depend on the disposition of the *demos*. According to Lincoln, the endpoint of this erosion of confidence will be regime change. Left unopposed, mob rule results in the overthrow of popular government. The really dangerous opportunists are not the petty criminals but the tyrannically inclined. Lincoln warns of "men of sufficient talent and ambition" who will "seize the opportunity" and "strike the blow" against free institutions. Sadly, they will be aided by the decent folks who, in troubled times, look to the strongman for deliverance. "We the People" become willing to trade anarchic liberty for despotic security, or at least the demagogic promise of it. Without being classically schooled, Lincoln seems to have discovered the disintegrative trajectory of extreme democracy first diagnosed by Plato and Aristotle.

Only now, at the conclusion of this long, long paragraph, does Lincoln allude to the event closest to home, the 1837 killing of the abolitionist editor Elijah Lovejoy in Alton, Illinois:

> whenever the vicious portion of population shall be permitted to gather in bands of hundreds and thousands, and burn churches, ravage and rob provision stores, throw printing presses into rivers, shoot editors, and hang and burn

obnoxious persons at pleasure, and with impunity; depend
on it, this Government cannot last.

If the audience has listened, they might be inclined to react to
current events with a little less knee-jerk fervor, whether pro-
Lovejoy or anti-Lovejoy. Their viewpoint has been shifted from
the immediate to the long-term, as well as from the narrowly
partisan to the public-spirited. Aware of the link between disregard for the law and the destruction of our political institutions,
they will count themselves among those "best citizens" who
can, because they foresee the danger, also act to avert this crisis
of popular government.

The paragraph in which Lincoln sketches this downward
spiral is by far the longest of the speech. Lincoln apparently
never got the memo about standard paragraph length. Whether
measured by sentences or words, his paragraphs vary widely,
almost wildly, providing clues to the work's structure and his intentions. Of the Lyceum's twenty-four paragraphs, fully a third
of them (paragraphs 1, 8, 11, 13, 18, 19, 21, and 24) are only one
sentence in length. By contrast, the two longest, paragraphs 9
and 17, are twenty sentences (719 words) and thirty-one sentences (590 words). Why might he squeeze all this into one paragraph? My hunch is that by proceeding without a breather and
by not allotting each indirect consequence its own paragraph,
Lincoln implies that all follows logically and inevitably from
that initial disregard of the law. Thus, the one-sentence paragraph (the shortest of the eight one-sentence paragraphs) that
soon follows this longest paragraph declares, "Here then, is **one
point** at which danger may be expected." Yet, this also means
that counter-action is straightforward, since it need only address

this "one point." Lincoln does not recommend a multi-faceted plan involving, say, prosecution of the culprits, a plea for greater civility, a call for journalistic accuracy, and a legislative initiative of some kind. Instead, he says,

> The answer is simple. Let every American, every lover of liberty, every well wisher to his posterity, swear by the blood of the Revolution, never to violate in the least particular, the laws of the country; and never to tolerate their violation by others.

The solution is absolute law-abidingness. And really more than that: not only must there be the action of obedience, but obedience should flow from an underlying attitude or "state of feeling." Democratic citizens should obey not out of fear but out of reverence. Indeed, Lincoln demands that "reverence for the laws . . . become the *political religion* of the nation." His solution is radical in that it goes to the root cause of the trouble, "the increasing disregard for law." Reverence uproots disrespect and thereby negates both the direct and indirect consequences of mob rule. The logic of paragraph 9 has revealed the imperative of law-abidingness, but Lincoln is aware that reason alone will not secure the required obedience. Echoing Aristotle (and I suppose the entire canon of wisdom literature), he highlights the role of habituation and piety in shaping a deferential attitude toward the law. Reverence depends on acculturation, hence the crucial role Lincoln assigns to mothers, teachers, and preachers.

There is precedent for this emphasis not only among the ancients but also within the American tradition. After all, that same Publius who in Federalist 51 spoke of relying on "opposite and rival interests" to take the place of "better motives" (they being always in short supply) had also spoken, two papers earlier, of his hope that the Constitution would be venerated. In Federalist 49, Publius described "reverence for the laws" as a salutary prejudice that buttresses the constitutional structure. Lincoln's call, however, seems to go further, at least in its appropriation of religious language for political purposes. He endows democratic theory, which establishes the binding character of consent-based law, with a sacred character:

> And, in short, let it [reverence for the laws] become the *political religion* of the nation; and let the old and the young, the rich and the poor, the grave and the gay, of all sexes and tongues, and colors and conditions, sacrifice unceasingly upon its altars.

DISOBEDIENCE: ALWAYS UNCIVIL OR SOMETIMES CIVIL?

And yet we might wonder whether there are not some exceptions to this first commandment. Perhaps the listing of worshippers, which might seem to be high-toned filler, is worth a closer look. The imperative applies to every American, of whatever age (old or young), economic status (rich or poor), temperament (grave or gay), of whatever sex (interesting that he implies there might be more than two), and of whatever heritage (as this is a nation of immigrants). He concludes with the two most interesting categories: those belonging to all "colors and conditions." Does the demand to revere the Constitution and laws apply to Blacks in America? Surely they are within the orbit of all colors. Does it then apply to those Black persons who find themselves in a condition of slavery as well as to those in a condition of freedom? How could it? For the slaves themselves, doesn't their natural right to liberty invalidate the man-made law establishing property in man? Aren't the slaves within their rights to attempt escape? Aren't they even within their rights to murder their master in his bed (especially if the master has left his own bed and entered theirs)? Despite being counted in the census of the population as three-fifths of a free person for purposes of representation, the slaves exist entirely outside the bounds of consent. We know that slave masters taught a quietistic version of Christianity to their human chattels: "slaves, obey your masters."[13] However, an American political religion sworn upon "the blood of the Revolution" could never demand or justify the obedience of enslaved persons. Thomas Jefferson had been utterly frank on this point. In his *Notes on the State of Virginia*, he pointed out that although slaves constituted one-half the citizens of his state, they could not be expected to have any *amor patriae*. Moreover, should they exercise their natural right of revolution, God would be on their side: "The Almighty has no attribute which can take side with us," said the slaveholder Jefferson, "in such a contest." All that Lincoln ever wrote about the Declaration of Independence indicates that he subscribes to this idea of pre-political natural rights and its by-any-means-necessary ethos. His call for a political religion of law-abidingness must have application to free citizens only. In effect, slaves remain in a state of war vis-à-vis their oppressors.

But even this acknowledgement that slaves don't fit within the designation "every American" doesn't resolve all the difficulties

in combining respect for law with a teaching that enshrines revolutionary resistance to violations of rights. What, for instance,
is the obligation of the friends of the slaves among the citizens?
How much must they "sacrifice" upon the altar of the law? Lincoln acknowledges the problem. Law at its best seeks justice,
but it is never identical to justice; moreover, sometimes law is
used to establish and maintain injustice. What then?

> When I so pressingly urge a strict observance of all the laws,
> let me not be understood as saying there are no bad laws . . .
> I mean to say no such thing.

Lincoln had more experience than we have of bad laws; not only
was slavery legal in half the states of the union, but the entire
nation was under a constitutional obligation to return fugitive
slaves to bondage. In an 1855 letter to his slaveholding friend
Joshua Speed, Lincoln describes the terrible sight of slaves being
"hunted down, and caught, and carried back to their stripes, and
unrewarded toils; but," he says, "I bite my lip and keep quiet."
He warns Speed that southerners should not be oblivious to
the moral and emotional toll exacted by this duty: "You ought
rather to appreciate how much the great body of the Northern
people do crucify their feelings, in order to maintain their loyalty to the Constitution and the Union." Comparing obedience
to the fugitive slave clause to a crucifixion, Lincoln stresses the
agony of compliance. The slaves are not the only sufferers. In
this one regard at least, the Constitution required the sacrifice of
one's moral and humane sentiments. In the Peoria Address, Lincoln will testify to the obnoxiousness of the three-fifths clause
as well, describing it as "manifestly unfair" and derogatory to

his "sacred rights" as an equal citizen (since the political effect of the three-fifths clause is to inflate the institutional weight of every white voter in the slaveholding states).

Lincoln is delivering a hard lesson in democratic theory. For citizens, there is no option of "civil" disobedience. All disobedience is uncivil and destructive of civil government. There is, of course, a right of revolution, but short of that exigency there is only acknowledgement of the majority's legitimate power through its ballots to determine the motion of the body politic. It is not that the majority is always right (it frequently is not), but the majority does have rightful authority—an authority that is itself grounded in the truth of natural equality and its logical corollary, government by consent. Offering a glimmer of hope and change, Lincoln points out that there is a democratic mechanism for addressing the problem of bad law: "bad laws, if they exist, should be repealed as soon as possible"; yet he immediately repeats the desideratum "still while they continue in force, for the sake of example, they should be religiously observed."

Martin Luther King, Jr., influenced in part by the antinomianism of Henry David Thoreau's "Civil Disobedience" (1849), famously argued that one can show respect for law (and speed the repeal of bad law) by means of a specific mode of lawbreaking. In his "Letter from a Birmingham Jail" (1963), King declares,

One who breaks an unjust law must do it *openly, lovingly* . . . , and with a willingness to accept the penalty. I submit that an individual who breaks a law that conscience tells him is unjust, and willingly accepts the penalty by staying in jail to arouse the conscience of the community over its injustice, is in reality expressing the very highest respect for law.[14]

Abraham Lincoln and Martin Luther King, Jr., are often viewed as our nation's greatest moral lights. Yet, they fundamentally disagree on this foundational question of the nature of citizenship and the relationship between law and justice. There is probably no better exercise for every American than to read Lincoln's Lyceum and King's "Letter" side by side, making a good faith effort to suspend one's biases (which I suspect are usually on the side of King) so as to test the logic of the two positions.

For Lincoln, the choice is limited to the ballot or the bullet, where "ballot" is a kind of shorthand not just for the elective franchise but for the myriad tools of democratic persuasion: free speech, free press, the rights of assembly and petition, and access to the courts (including the powerful tactic implicit within judicial review of testing the constitutionality of local, state, and federal laws). But outright nullification, no matter how nonviolent, is impermissible, whether by Thoreau's "minority of one" or John C. Calhoun's minority of South Carolina, which had proclaimed a "right of state interposition" against federal laws that it regarded as unjust and discriminatory. While there is much to celebrate in King's legacy, it still seems to me an open question whether his advocacy of "civil disobedience" has not, as Lincoln would have predicted, eroded respect for the rule of law. Could the struggle for civil rights have been conducted exclusively through constitutionally prescribed methods? In considering this, it is extraordinarily important to remember that no lawbreaking was involved in most of the techniques and activities of the movement. The ingenious battle in the courts waged by the NAACP, the dangerous work of voter registration in the South, the Montgomery bus boycott, and similar heroic instances of nonviolent mass protest—all were fully within the law. At the least one might say that the popularity of King's essay, which most students read at some point in their schooling, has inflated the role that disobedience played in bringing about positive social change, both in King's endeavors and in the larger enterprise.

One might also consider whether King's strictures on the allowable mode of lawbreaking (open, loving, and penalty-accepting) would have worked in Lincoln's day against the Fugitive Slave Law. That law was resisted, but the Underground Railroad operated, by necessity, in secret. The aim, of course, was not really the repeal of the law; it was simply rescue and the spiriting to freedom of as many slaves as possible. Frederick Douglass, who was involved in these activities, also wrote an editorial in 1854 titled "Is It Right and Wise to Kill a Kidnapper?," in which he called for a more open and dramatic form of resistance. Arguing that the ravenous slave-catchers had forfeited their right to life by their assault on those who were pursuing their own right to liberty, and further that since the government was failing in its duty to protect the innocent, either the slave "or his friends" might act in his defense, meting out "bloody death" to those engaged in the "infernal business." (Similar arguments have been made since *Roe v. Wade*, attempting to justify the targeting of abortionists.) It should be noted that Douglass regarded the 1850 Fugitive Slave Act as unconstitutional since he did not read the Constitution's language of "persons held to service or labor" as having any reference to slaves. His strict construction of the document (if it doesn't say "slave" it doesn't mean "slave") led him to surmise that this clause applied only to indentured servants who had signed labor contracts and thus could be held to their terms of service. Lincoln, by contrast, did believe there was a constitutional obligation to return escaped

slaves, for as he argued in the First Inaugural, "the intention of
the law-giver is the law." One can't help wondering, though,
what Lincoln would have done had the runaway appeared at his
own door. Would he have found a way to turn the blind eye of
justice upon the situation rather than the peering eye of the law?

Even without getting into hermeneutic quarrels over constitutional interpretation, Douglass's endorsement of violence
should be a voice in this discussion. Douglass's argument is the
precursor of Malcolm X's assertion that "when our people are
being bitten by dogs, they are within their rights to kill those
dogs." Malcolm X understood the Lockean logic. Legitimate
government based on a free ballot binds the individual to obedience; illegitimate government does not. The Lockean corrective
to governmental abuse is revolution—or at least a potent threat
of revolution. As Malcolm X put it: "It'll be Molotov cocktails
this month, hand grenades next month, and something else next
month. It'll be ballots, or it'll be bullets. It'll be liberty, or it will be
death." His incendiary language notwithstanding, he was careful
to present this violence in the context of justifiable self-defense:
"I don't mean go out and get violent; but at the same time you
should never be nonviolent unless you run into some nonvio-
lence." It is often said that Malcolm X was useful to the cause of
racial justice because his extremism frightened white Americans
into accepting reforms they otherwise wouldn't have—in other
words, Malcolm played bad cop to Martin's good cop. But instead
of this blithe historicist justification, perhaps we should consider
the possibility that elements of Malcolm X's radicalism were in
fact superior, on their own terms, because they held true to the
nation's foundations and were, in the long run, less dangerous.
Malcolm X is not antinomian in the way that King is. As Lincoln

argued in the Lyceum Address, antinomianism (which acknowledges no authority other than the individual conscience) threat-
ens not just law and order but, more profoundly, law and justice.
While one might disagree with Malcolm X's assertion that Blacks
in America were nothing more than "victims of Americanism,"
his classic formulation of the issue—"in 1964, it's the ballot or
the bullet"—accords with the understanding of John Locke, the
American founders, and Abraham Lincoln.[15]

ANOTHER TOUGH CASE

It is tempting to try to lessen the gulf between Lincoln's reverential obedience and King's reverential disobedience by citing Lincoln's apparent qualification of his argument in paragraph 14:
"let them, if not too intolerable, be borne with." Does this caveat open some space for selective disobedience to laws that are
"too intolerable"? This search for wiggle room in Lincoln's edict
involves, I believe, a misreading of his words. It ignores a crucial distinction that Lincoln draws between two types of challenging situations. Sometimes we are confronted with bad laws;
other times we encounter a situation where there is, as yet, no
law on a subject. Let's look again at the passage: "let me not be
understood as saying there are no bad laws, **nor** that grievances
may not arise, for the redress of which, no legal provisions have
been made." These are distinct cases. With respect to the first
case, that of bad laws, Lincoln insists "they must be religiously
observed" (until repealed). And we have already noted he does
not make an exception for the worst imaginable law, the Fugitive
Slave Law of 1850, which not only provided for the return of
escaped slaves but, by unfair provisions, left free Blacks exposed

to kidnappers.[16] When he turns to the second situation, Lincoln says, "So also in **unprovided cases**. If such arise, let proper legal provisions be made for them with the least possible delay; but, till then, let them, if not too intolerable, be borne with." Grammar comes to our aid in understanding what Lincoln has said. The "them" that might be "too intolerable" are not bad laws but "unprovided cases," meaning behavior or activity that occasions strong public hostility but is not illegal, or at least not yet illegal. Human wrongdoing is endlessly inventive and often outstrips the imaginative foresight of the law, as we have seen in our own time with the perverse phenomenon of consensual homicide or consensual abuse, requiring additional refinement of the law.

But this is not the sort of example that Lincoln offers. The one and only example he mentions, in paragraph 15, is "the promulgation of abolitionism"—an unprovided case about which many Americans were then aggrieved, so aggrieved that they sought to silence the vituperative speech of the abolitionists by destroying their printing presses and shooting their publishers. For the first time in the address, slavery takes center stage. Of course, it has been a persistent subtext throughout. We could go back to Lincoln's initial description of the mob outrages, which he insisted were not sectional in character:

> They have pervaded the country, from New England to Louisiana;—they are neither peculiar to the eternal snows of the former, nor the burning suns of the latter;—they are not the creature of climate—neither are they confined to the slave-holding, or the non-slave-holding States. Alike, they spring up among the pleasure hunting masters of Southern slaves, and the order loving citizens of the land of steady habits.

This is carefully composed; while insisting that mob rule is a national problem, Lincoln manages to highlight key sectional differences. There is certainly no moral equivalence here. The north has "citizens" not "masters," who love "order" not "pleasure," and whose institutions involve commerce and other "steady habits" rather than the daily exercise of tyranny over "slaves." It is also telling that Lincoln drew his two main examples of mob outbreaks from two slave states (Mississippi and Missouri), and both involved, at least in part, the targeting of Blacks. Meanwhile, the Illinois case referred to obliquely in paragraph 9 (by the mention of "the vicious portion of population" being permitted to "shoot editors") is only now in paragraph 15 made thematic, as Lincoln introduces "the promulgation of abolitionism" as an instance of a "grievance."

Throughout the nation, mob actions against the hated abolitionists were being catalyzed by this "unprovided case" the fact that there was no explicit law either protecting or banning abolitionism. Lincoln looked for a way of broaching the issue without inflaming things further. Just as he did not defend the gamblers who were the victims of mob punishment, he was not going to irritate his audience by defending the abolitionists. Of course, beneath the anger *of* the abolitionists and the anger *at* the abolitionists lies the issue of slavery itself. Lincoln, however, does not directly address either abolitionism or slavery. Indeed, he quite rigorously withholds his own judgment of those matters. For the moment at least, he focuses not on abolition doctrine but on its vocalization—its promulgation—about which he says, "one of two positions is necessarily true": either "the thing is right within itself, and therefore deserves the protection of all law and all good citizens; or, it is wrong, and therefore proper to be prohibited by legal enactments." Lincoln raises the question of the rightness or wrongness of its promulgation as a topic that ought to be discussed and decided. He is trying to create space for reasoned public deliberation that would elevate principles over partisanship. "Good citizens" must think these things through.

One way of addressing the issue would be to approach it as a matter of free speech. Let's take a case that has arisen in our times: the promulgation of Nazism. Nazism is wrong; and one hopes and prays that the American public recognizes it as wrong. Even so, do its advocates have a right to promulgate their wrong teaching (and even to march in Skokie)? In Lincoln's day, unfortunately, the disfavored speech was, in many places, that of the abolitionists. Yet, it might be possible to persuade even those who despised the abolitionists as fanatics that the promulgation of abolitionism is constitutionally protected speech. But it is also possible that in considering whether the promulgation of abolitionism is right or wrong, one would be led to ask whether abolitionist doctrine is right or wrong. Pursuing that inquiry would eventually bring one to the most fundamental question of whether slavery is right or wrong. In its broadest contours, the question of the legitimacy of abolitionism would require the public to reflect on both the moral and the constitutional status of slavery, including the possibility of a disjunction between those two. When Lincoln insists that "there is no grievance that is a fit object of redress by mob law," he is attempting to shift the conflict into the channels of democratic debate and away from the dangerous flood plains of "interposition." Note that in using this loaded word, "interposition," Lincoln subtly but deliberately links Calhoun's South Carolina heresy to mob law. Calhoun's doctrine of nullification, whereby each state was to have the right to decide the constitutionality of federal laws for itself, was also called state interposition. By using the word here, Lincoln indicates that "interposition" is a version of anti-constitutional anarchy. The same is true of Thoreau's conscientious "interposition," where the most woke decides for herself which laws to accept as binding.

By the way, Lincoln had already formulated his own answers to these three interrelated questions of right and wrong (slavery, abolitionism, and its promulgation) in his 1837 Protest against the Illinois legislature's Anti-Abolition Resolutions. There he began by stating his belief that "the institution of slavery is founded on both injustice and bad policy," but also that "the promulgation of abolition doctrines tends rather to increase than to abate its [slavery's] evils." Agreeing with the abolitionists about the wrongfulness of slavery, Lincoln nonetheless separates himself from elements both of their doctrine (such as their disdain for constitutionalism) and of their antipathetic mode of presentation. Without interfering with their right to speak, publish, and assemble, he suggests that those who care about the anti-slavery cause ought to take care not to aggravate the evil they would extirpate. This is a message he will deliver more fully in his 1842 Temperance Address, where he sketches his theory of rhetoric, especially the reasons to avoid "the thundering tones of anathema and denunciation."

Before leaving the realm of "unprovided cases," we might wonder what might count for Lincoln as a "too intolerable" unprovided case—always remembering, though, that "there is no grievance that is a fit object of redress by mob law." I can think of one example from the war years. In May 1864, Lincoln met the widow of a white officer who had died at Fort Pillow commanding African American troops.[17] She let him know that since slaves had not been allowed to marry, the widows and orphans of many fallen soldiers were not entitled to federal benefits. For Lincoln, it seems this was an instance of an unprovided case being too grievous to be permitted to stand. He suggested to Charles Sumner that "widows and children *in fact*, of colored soldiers who fall in our service, be placed in law, the same as if their marriages were legal, so that they can have the benefit of the provisions made the widows & children of white soldiers." Lincoln's approach involved making legislative provision for an unprovided case, but interestingly it was a provision that operated retroactively, proceeding "as if" there had been a legal marriage. It overrode the strict letter of the law in the direction of equity and charity.

"WHAT, ME WORRY?"

It might seem that the Lyceum Address should end here at paragraph 15. The speaker has diagnosed the problem, presented its solution, evaluated possible exceptions, and concluded with the ringing declaration that "the interposition of mob law" is never "necessary, justifiable, or excusable." Lincoln, however, pursuing his dialogue with the audience, has an imagined interlocutor engage in a different sort of interposition, interrupting with a flurry of questions:

> But, it may be asked, why suppose danger to our political institutions? Have we not preserved them for more than fifty years? And why may we not for fifty times as long?

The questions are prompted, perhaps, by resistance to the rigor of Lincoln's solution. Do we really need to be so all-fired virtuous? Even if the audience is now prepared to admit that the lawbreaking has gotten a little out of hand, is total abstinence the only answer? Like the drinker who has been imbibing every day for years but can't conceive of cirrhosis, the American people are disinclined to accept what the projection into the future, based on their present behavior, looks like. For Lincoln's intervention to be successful, he must confront a deeper problem. Beneath the surface ferment of the present moment, there lies a cavalier complacency about the future.

Precisely this had been the line taken by Martin Van Buren in his Inaugural, delivered in March 1837. As the first president whose birth postdated the revolution, he acknowledged belonging to "a later age" than those "earliest and firmest pillars of the Republic." Nonetheless, Van Buren saw no cause for generational foreboding. His confidence was based on a detailed survey of the fears that had been expressed at the time of the founding—all now, he announced in his inaugural, wonderfully disproved. Men then had worried that citizens would not submit to the requisite levels of taxation; they worried that once George Washington passed from the scene, factionalism would damage the union; they worried that municipal law would not be dutifully obeyed; they worried that popular government would not be strong or quick enough to handle emergencies; they worried about the expansive and expanding size of the republic; they worried about the proper balance of power between federal and state authorities; and finally, "the last, perhaps the greatest, of the prominent sources of discord and disaster supposed to lurk in our political condition was the institution of

domestic slavery." With respect to this last, Van Buren admitted that "recent events" have displayed "the violence of excited
passions." However, he placed the blame for these "terrifying
instances of local violence" squarely on the initiators of "dangerous agitation." With the abolitionists clearly in mind, Van
Buren said that "a reckless disregard of the consequences of
their conduct has exposed individuals to popular indignation"—
basically, people like Lovejoy got what was coming to them. To
lay to rest "the agitation of this subject," Van Buren called for a
return to the "delicacy" and "forbearance" of the founders. But
for him the spirit of civility and compromise was to flow in one
direction only. Deference, in word and deed, must be accorded
the sensitivities of the slaveholders. (Sensitivity training is never
impartial.)

With respect to the policy question of the day, Van Buren
declared himself "the inflexible and uncompromising opponent
of every attempt on the part of Congress to abolish slavery in
the District of Columbia against the wishes of the slaveholding
States." By contrast, Lincoln in his 1837 Protest made clear that
Congress had sole constitutional power over the federal district
and could act to abolish slavery there, although he also advised
that the power should be tempered by respect for the consent
of the people of the District.[18] He did not, however, extend that
veto power to the slaveholding states or even that subset of slaveholding states, Maryland and Virginia, that had ceded the land
out of which the District was created. Although a New Yorker,
Van Buren further promised the American people "to resist the
slightest interference with it [slavery] in the States where it exists." In his 1837 Protest, Lincoln had said only that Congress
had "no power, under the constitution, to interfere with the

institution of slavery in the different States." Van Buren's full-throated determination to defend the slaveholding interest fits perfectly with his appeal for a speech code of sorts, whereby all citizens censor language that might perturb the slaveholders. As we have seen, Lincoln's approach was the opposite. Rather than silencing dissent under the misnomer of "fraternal feeling," he encouraged truly civil discourse, placing front and center the need for shared moral inquiry.

Van Buren's Inaugural was intended to be reassuring. Since no danger ahead could be worse than the dangers already conquered, Americans could simply trust to time:

> We have seen time gradually dispel every unfavorable foreboding and our Constitution surmount every adverse circumstance dreaded at the outset as beyond control. Present excitement will at all times magnify present dangers, but true philosophy must teach us that none more threatening than the past can remain to be overcome; and we ought (for we have just reason) to entertain an abiding confidence in the stability of our institutions and an entire conviction that if administered in the true form, character, and spirit in which they were established they are abundantly adequate to preserve to us and our children the rich blessings already derived from them, to make our beloved land for a thousand generations that chosen spot where happiness springs from a perfect equality of political rights.

Lincoln's ultimate aim in the Lyceum Address is to dispel this democratic complacency—a complacency that would, despite its aura of patriotism, "blow out the moral lights around us" (this was a favorite phrase of Lincoln's, borrowed from Henry Clay). Lincoln imitates Van Buren by engaging in an act of retrospection, but his look back, which entails a startling reconsideration of the founding generation, yields a very different prospect. From Van Buren's list of seven founding-era fears (all proven groundless, according to him), Lincoln zeroes in on the third (the disregard for law) and links it to the seventh (slavery). Then, in the final section of the speech, from paragraphs 16 through 24, he introduces unforeseen causes for concern, "causes, dangerous in their tendency, which have not existed heretofore."

THE LION-KING

In the first half of the speech, devoted to the present danger of mob rule, human beings had been divided between the lawless and the law-abiding, between "the vicious portion of population" and "the best citizens." Yet, Lincoln had also mentioned "men of sufficient talent and ambition" waiting in the wings to overturn the political order. Picking up on that hint, Lincoln now delves into that ancient staple of political thought: the distinction between the few and the many, including how that distinction affected the nation's founding and how it will affect the future. Lincoln's initial view of the founding generation, back in paragraph 2, had spoken simply of a "hardy, brave, and patriotic . . . race of ancestors." On reconsideration, however, Lincoln reveals that the ancestors were composed of two distinct human types, possessing divergent motives. Those two sets of animating passions, however, turn out to be equally questionable. On Lincoln's retelling, the success of the national experiment can be traced to some less-than-admirable traits. In 1776, the few were avid for "celebrity and fame, and distinction," while the many were driven by "deep rooted principles of *hate*, and the powerful motive of *revenge*," directed exclusively against the British. Thus, the self-serving passions of all were happily, but coincidentally, mustered for the cause of civil and religious liberty.

Examining the few, Lincoln offers metaphors—drawn from the realms of science, agriculture, and architecture—to understand "their ruling passion." Like mathematicians, the founders were attracted to an unproven proposition, namely *"the capability of a people to govern themselves."* What will remain to be accomplished by persons of the founding type born after the founding? They will be like reapers in the fields of glory not content with the gleanings, or like master builders not content to serve as custodians in the house erected by the fathers. The existence of this overweening and aggrieved ambition seems to be a new form of an "unprovided case." Lincoln calls it "a probable case."

Yet didn't the founders anticipate and provide scope for the aspiring few? Certainly, they were aware of the power latent in the love of fame. Alexander Hamilton, in Federalist 72, called it "the ruling passion of the noblest minds." The whole ingenious, complicated structure of separated powers, supplemented with checks and balances, set in a large, compound republic divided into national and state levels, is meant to meet this danger. It does so not by suppressing ambition but by harnessing it to the duties of office and the public good. James Madison in Federalist 51 described the strategy: "Ambition must be made to counteract ambition." Well-aware of these mechanisms, Lincoln in fact finds them reliable for the "many great and good men . . . whose ambition would aspire to nothing beyond a seat in Congress, a gubernatorial or a presidential chair." But he insists there are others (maybe just one) for whom even the highest office would be small potatoes. "Such a one" cannot be contained within the horizon of the regime. He is quite literally out-standing. In giving historical examples of republic-destroying builders of empire, Lincoln switches the metaphor from human to beast, stating that the likes of Alexander, Caesar, and Napoleon belong to *"the family of the lion, or the tribe of the eagle."*[19] A natural predator behaves as if entitled to take what it likes. Significantly, there follows a sequence of five sentences all beginning with "It" as the pronoun for this man-beast, this entity of "towering genius." Denying the equality premise of the Declaration, the lion-king would presumably scorn the indignity of soliciting votes from the rabbits. And yet, according to Lincoln, the only restraint upon this incipient tyrant must come from the concerted resistance of the prey—a.k.a., the people.

Thomas Jefferson, too, had counted more on the character of the people than the structure of the government, frequently expressing the hope that Americans, once properly educated, could be trusted to separate the meritorious from the meretricious, or, as he put it in his epistolary exchange with John Adams, "the natural aristocrats" from the "pseudalists." Lincoln, however, has ratcheted up the difficulty, since these lion-like ones, although not Jefferson's "really good and wise" (who merit the suffrage of their fellows), are not exactly frauds or mere oligarchs, either. They are, in some sense, the real deal, even if, in the final analysis, they are not as different from other human beings as they think they are. Indicative of their conceit is the fact that the very question the lion in the fable roars at the hares when he dismisses their harangue for equality—"where are your claws and teeth?"—could just as legitimately be asked by the demos of the aspiring tyrant when he asserts that he is so superior as to be a law onto himself. Whereas Jefferson identifies natural aristocrats by their virtue (as does Aristotle), Lincoln's "towering genius" is morally neutral, a sheer opportunist, "emancipating slaves, or enslaving freemen" with about equal alacrity. This, by the way, is the fourth and final appearance of the word "slave" in the Lyceum Address.

Not surprisingly, given Lincoln's later career as the "Great Emancipator," this passage has occasioned much speculation as to whether Lincoln himself belongs to the type. Why should Lincoln remain true to republicanism if leonine glory is within his grasp? And did he remain true? There have always been those who thought he did not—*sic semper tyrannis* was the cry of the assassin John Wilkes Booth. These are inquiries for later, but for now it might just be noted that it is odd to warn people of the threat you yourself pose. Of course, such a warning might be a particularly clever ruse, designed to disarm the people's suspicions, but, if so, it smacks more of the fox than of the lion. No actual lion employs rhetoric. While politics is not reduceable to rhetoric, the ubiquity of its presence—the fact that every human ruler must attempt persuasive speech—indicates the limits of the lion metaphor.

AN ALTERNATIVE TO BLOODY SCENES

Lincoln does more than warn against a coming Napoleon. He summons the people, letting them know they will need three things to frustrate a designing tyrant. Resistance "will require the people to be united with each other, attached to the government and laws, and generally intelligent." Were these three qualities in evidence during the original era of resistance to tyranny, or were they unnecessary then? Lincoln launches another surprising reassessment of the founding generation, one focused on ordinary folks rather than the few glory-seekers. In order to make his point about changed circumstances, Lincoln in paragraph 20 explains what really motivated that "*once* hardy, brave, and patriotic, but *now* lamented and departed race of ancestors," which he had so fulsomely praised back in paragraph 2. Italicizing the same words in these widely separated paragraphs, Lincoln reveals that the "*once* . . . patriotic, . . . *now* lamented . . . ancestors" were driven by a factor "which *once was*; but which, to the same extent, is *now no more*," namely, "the powerful influence which the interesting scenes of the revolution had upon the *passions* of the people as distinguished from their judgment." The people were riled up. As he says in the Temperance Address, the political revolution of '76 "swam in blood and rode on fire." The stirring spectacles of the fight for independence had salutary effects, suppressing certain negative passions, like "jealousy, envy, and avarice," and putting others, especially "*hate*" and "*revenge*," to good purpose. Lincoln is coldly and brutally honest: the patriotism and bravery we celebrate were forged from "the basest principles of our nature." The problem of the American future is that this spectacular source of unity "*must fade, is fading, has faded.*"

Approaching the close of his address, Lincoln circles back to the twin themes of the speech's opening: time and text. Remember that Lincoln had earlier described his generation's task as the act of transmitting their inheritance "undecayed by **the**

lapse of time." In paragraph 22, he reveals the inevitability of those impassioning scenes of the revolution becoming "more dim by **the lapse of time**." The project of perpetuation must confront the fleeting nature of both passion and memory. To explore this, Lincoln considers different types of reading—some of which involve reading things other than books—as antidotes to the unreliability of memory. Lincoln movingly describes the *"living history"* embodied in the veterans of the Revolutionary War. So long as those heroes live, the "scenes of the revolution" remain alive through them. The authenticity of their witness is found "in the limbs mangled, in the scars of wounds received." This *"living history"* had the great advantage that it "could be read and understood alike by all, the wise and the ignorant, the learned and the unlearned." In other words, "general intelligence" and "judgment" on the part of the people were not required. However, the great disadvantage is that this form of text, written in flesh, is mortal. With more than half a century having passed since the war's end, Lincoln announces, *"those* histories are gone. They *can* be read no more forever."

Lincoln seeks a text that is impervious to the "silent artillery of time." His standards are high. He does not seem at all confident that the scenes of the revolution, when translated into the written word of historical accounts, will be sufficient to animate patriotic attachment. Stating his "hope" that the revolutionary stories "will be read of, and recounted, so long as the bible shall be read," he nonetheless adds, "but even granting that they will, their influence *cannot be* what it heretofore has been." The early fervor cools. Once again, Lincoln's practice of comparing politics to religion carries startling implications. Do his doubts about the perdurance of historical memory apply not only to the scenes of the revolution but also to those of the Bible? He implies as much. When "the Word was made flesh, and dwelt among us," as John 1:14 put it, that was *"living history."* Are those scenes not "so vividly felt" now that the bearer of the wounds and the disciples who saw the wounds are gone? For Christians, perhaps the presence of the Holy Spirit makes up for that loss of direct contact. Could there be a political equivalent, a source of abiding, never-failing spirit?

A few years before the Lyceum Address, when he first ran for political office in Sangamo County, Lincoln had endorsed the needfulness of universal literacy. Declaring education "the most important subject which we as a people can be engaged in," he detailed the political and personal significance of book learning. Knowledge of comparative political history teaches "the value of our free institutions" and "being able to read the scriptures and other works, both of a religious and moral nature," yields "advantages and satisfactions." The Lyceum Address is compatible with this 1832 Sangamo statement, but it takes the further step of discriminating among genres. Lincoln now disparages those books that depend on the evocation of feeling or pathos. The immediacy of *"living history"* can never be captured through the medium of the history books. Earnestly recounting "the scenes of the revolution" will not guarantee perpetuation. Of course, this is a rather disheartening message to all those today who hope that renewed attention to the teaching of history will have good civic effects.

As an aside, we might just wonder why Lincoln, who excelled at telling stories, would downplay the efficacy of storytelling. It's probably important to remember that Lincoln specialized in humorous tales and jokes. Humor relies on logic to a much greater degree than do other modes of storytelling, whether historical or poetical (like epic, tragedy, and lyric). Comedy is almost the antithesis of pathos. It builds distance and objectivity rather than identification. It capitalizes on stereotypes: "A Norwegian and a Swede walk into a bar . . ."; "How many professors does it take to screw in a lightbulb?" Wit works by the surprise of juxtaposition and disproportion. It exploits the oddities of language, as with puns and double entendre. Humor is an exercise of the mind, not the heart.

It is to the mind that Lincoln turns for a more lasting alternative to "the scenes of the revolution." His solution to both present and future dangers involves a different type of text altogether. Lincoln encourages an unmediated attachment to the primary texts, not the textbooks, not the stories of living history "in the form of a husband, a father, a son or a brother," but the fundamental charters that govern communal life. This is not at odds with what he will say at Trenton in 1861 about his youthful reading of *The Life of Washington*. While his imagination had been stirred by Weems's account of the battle of Trenton, he also said that he thought, "boy even though I was," that behind the struggle was "the original idea," the principle that (in part, at least, for we can't forget the baser props and passions) motivated the willingness to bear such hardship. In the Lyceum Address, Lincoln argues that just as "the patriots of seventy-six" pledged themselves to the support of a text, the Declaration of Independence, his generation should swear an oath (and a blood oath, at that) to other texts, "the Constitution and Laws." Lincoln always pushes his analysis toward the discovery of principles or the recovery of forgotten principles. He is a textual fundamentalist, and he was so from the beginning.

What does it mean to be a constitutional people? A nation founded upon a text has an ever-renewable resource for perpetuity not available to other nations. This might explain why, in that same Trenton speech, Lincoln called Americans an "almost chosen people," as if we are runners-up to the Jews, the original people of the Book. To be a constitutional people is to practice a particular conjugation of word and flesh, believing that the word can be made flesh. Lincoln's text-centered approach can be seen not only in the priority he assigns the Declaration and the Constitution but in his life-long study of the Bible. Although he avoided church membership and, for long stretches of his life, church attendance, he read the Bible regularly. Whatever the status of his faith—and that is a highly contested subject—Lincoln had more command of Scripture than any elected American leader before or since. The most remarkable display of his knowledge is his 1859 First Lecture on Discoveries and Inventions, where he traces the history of technology—and between the lines, the history of slavery—through three dozen Bible references.[20]

OUR ENEMY: PASSION

Having subjected the passions of the few and the many to this withering assessment, Lincoln's conclusion is emphatic: "Passion has helped us, but can do so no more. It will in future be our enemy." Like the demand for reverential obedience, this anti-passion message is hard for us to hear. Every graduation speech and self-help manual instructs: Find Your Passion, Live Your Passion. I suspect our contemporary fixation on passion is a response to our almost unlimited choices. Young people, especially advantaged young people, see an open vista and nothing external directing their choice. For most of human history, one's way of life was a given. Women had marriage and family; men followed the trade or profession of their fathers. With all limits removed (and aware that mere material success may not bring happiness), we now search for some compelling force, something unchosen that wells up and takes the decision out of our hands altogether. Of course, there was an older language that spoke of discerning one's vocation or finding a calling, but that involved subordination to a higher power; one answered His call. This should remind us that the original meaning of passion is "to suffer," as in the Passion of the Christ. Although the modern version is much attenuated, there is still a sense that in finding your passion, you find that for which you would put forth effort and make sacrifices (at the very least, the sacrifice of those other life options).

Yet this redefinition or repurposing of passion has a downside, especially for our politics. A passionate and impassioning politics is likely to be divisive. The passions Lincoln mentions, hate and revenge, are as deep-seated as their opposites. Sparking fear is probably easier than sparking joy. We celebrate passion—passion unmoored from notions of duty or piety or anything other than subjective desire—and then lament its negative consequences: hyper-partisanship, hate-filled invective, insufferable self-righteousness, and general nastiness.

Our contemporary bafflement at Lincoln's disapproval of passion is also a function of our less precise vocabulary. Whereas we sloppily treat words like "passion," "feeling," and "sentiment" as synonyms, Lincoln does not regard them as equivalent. He consistently uses "passion" to indicate negative "feelings" only.

By the way, this usage was not unique to Lincoln. Throughout their joint debates, Stephen Douglas ascribed a disreputable connotation to "passion," linking it to anarchy and violence. All Lincoln's references to passion are to the ill-tempered kind that sets groups against one another. This is clearly the case in the Lyceum Address and still true in 1861, when he concluded his First Inaugural with his most famous denigration of passion: "Though passion may have strained, it must not break our bonds of affection"—the affectional bonds here are not rooted in passion, only the stressors are. For Lincoln, "feeling" is the larger category. A word search of Lincoln's collected works shows that feelings might be "kind" or "unkind," "fraternal" or "harsh," "sincere" or "unpleasant." There are "Union feelings" and "feelings of indifference."

Although feeling creatures, human beings also possess judgment, which can be sound or unsound. Interestingly, Lincoln uses the word "sentiment" to describe what is created by the interaction of feeling and judgment. Sometimes the compound is quite unstable, as when one's hostile feelings are at odds with one's better judgment, or the reverse, when one's better feelings are at odds with one's corrupted judgment. Judgment and feeling can also be powerfully in accord. In his Cooper Union Address in 1859, Lincoln proclaimed, "There is a judgment and a feeling against slavery in this nation," warning southerners that they "cannot destroy that judgment and feeling—that sentiment—by breaking up the political organization which rallies around it." That anti-slavery sentiment, which was in some sense latent in the public since it was grounded in human nature itself and "the moral sentiment of mankind," nonetheless had to be awakened and solidified by political persuasion. Democratic persuasion involves appeals to both judgment and feeling but, according to Lincoln, should always avoid exciting passion.

From the Lyceum Address through to the Second Inaugural, Lincoln rejects attempts to impassion political life. He avoids making visceral appeals to hatred and revenge ("with malice toward none"). He is pretty skittish even about appeals to compassion. To be compassionate is to suffer along with the sufferer, but that quite naturally provokes anger at those who cause the suffering. While Lincoln certainly composed moving passages about the wrongfulness of slavery, in general he did not dwell on or try to evoke the horrors of the institution in the way that abolitionist orators did. Lincoln sought always to lift the slavery debate to the level of principle and unimpassioned reason, avoiding the dangerous ground of compassion, anger, and blame.

SOBER REASON

The Lyceum Address began by describing the task of the current generation as transmitting the "political edifice of liberty and equal rights . . . undecayed by the lapse of time." In paragraph 17 Lincoln indicated that the "props" that once supported this edifice "now are decayed, and crumbled away." Those old props were the passions of the few and the many during the revolutionary period. We might ask ourselves: If the attempt to establish the truth of the proposition of self-government depended on props, has the proposition really been proved? Lincoln grants that "it is understood to be a successful [experiment]" and, more emphatically, he says "they succeeded." Nonetheless, it seems that each generation must give its own "practical demonstration of the truth of a proposition." If the Lyceum Address has convinced us of anything, it is that maintenance differs from establishment. The temple of liberty must be outfitted anew, with pillars rather than props—pillars hewn from the more rot-resistant material of "sober reason."

Until reason presides over passion in the souls of Americans, the proposition is still unproven. Self-government in the collective depends on self-government within the self. There is no perpetuation without betterment.

What does betterment look like? What does it mean concretely to rely on reason? Lincoln says that reason can be "moulded" into three things: *general intelligence, sound morality* and, in particular, *a reverence for the constitution and laws.*" We see how the call for reverence, issued in paragraph 12, is now nested within this more comprehensive call for reason. In Lincoln's usage, reverence is not a passion. Political reverence is itself an instantiation of reason—a mold that reason can be poured into or a form that reason can take. To illustrate, think of what Lincoln said about the matrix of political reverence: "Let reverence for the laws, be breathed by every American mother, to the lisping babe, that prattles on her lap." Nature establishes what might be called "natural reverence." A child literally looks up, in love and fear, to its mother. Political reverence, however, must be deliberately incubated. Properly educated mothers can direct the child's reverential gaze toward the law, which has been adjudged worthy. Lincoln suggests incorporating this affectional element, subordinating it to the determinations of reason.

Note also that Lincoln's italicized list of three new pillars in his penultimate paragraph has some intriguing similarities with the list of three qualities the people must have in order to foil an aspiring tyrant, mentioned in paragraph 17. The parallelism can be seen by presenting the lists side by side and then determining the matching pairs.

List A (from paragraph 17) The Requisite Qualities of the People	List B (from paragraph 23) The New Pillars
1) united with each other	1′) *general intelligence*
2) attached to the government and laws	2′) *sound morality*
3) generally intelligent	3′) *a reverence for the constitution and laws*

"*General intelligence*" (1′) pairs with "generally intelligent" (3). And "*a reverence for the constitution and laws*" (3′) pairs with "attached to the government and laws" (2). But what about "*sound morality*" (2′)—how is it related to "united with each other" (1)? This less-obvious pairing is the kernel of Lincoln's reform. Whereas the original union was propped up by "the basest principles of our nature," in the future, the temple of liberty must be supported by (or unified around) a reason-based morality. President Van Buren had suggested a very different replacement pillar. Recommending in his 1837 Inaugural Address that Americans speak not a word in derogation of "domestic institutions which, unwisely disturbed, might endanger the harmony of the whole," Van Buren had constructed his new pillar out of the material of moral indifference—the very same material selected by Stephen Douglas for his legislative craftsmanship in the Kansas-Nebraska Act of 1854. In his 1837 Protest, Lincoln had already spelled out the alternative, namely unified agreement about the "injustice and bad policy" of the institution of slavery. Such foundational agreement would not resolve all disputes; but coupled with general intelligence and constitutional reverence, it would provide a legal, moral, and prudential way forward—a way that Lincoln painstakingly elaborated throughout the 1850s.

THE PAEAN TO WASHINGTON

According to Lincoln, these three reason-built pillars will yield three results: *general intelligence* will ensure "that we improved to the last," *sound morality* "that we remained free to the last," and *reverence for the constitution and laws* will mean in addition "that we revered his name to the last; that, during his long sleep, we permitted no hostile foot to pass over or desecrate his resting place." The final two sentences of the speech are rhetorically elaborate, as Lincoln now yokes the textual reverence he has been encouraging all along to reverence for a single individual— although he delays, and thereby heightens, the revelation of that person's identity. We learn of "his name," "his long sleep," and "his resting place" before we know who he is. When the absent one finally appears it is with a poetic flourish that imagines the promised resurrection of the nation's father. Blending the sacred and the patriotic, Lincoln envisions "our WASHINGTON" raised from the grave by "the last trump" and thus able to learn how his countrymen have fared (remaining free and improving—or not) over the years. The biblical reference is to 1st Corinthians 15:52, when "the dead shall be raised incorruptible" on the day of rapture. This second appearing of Washington depends, of course, on the Second Coming of Christ and the Christian promise of the resurrection of the body and the life everlasting.

In this peroration, Lincoln circles back to the end times that he hinted at in the speech's opening through the mention of "the latest generation that fate shall permit the world to know." Fate has now taken the form of Christian eschatology. Not only does Lincoln allude to the final victory over death, but the final one-sentence paragraph then repeats the thought with a this-worldly application by comparing the possible longevity of our political institutions to the staying power of "the only greater institution," which is to say, the Church. By ending the Lyceum Address with the direct quote from Matthew 16:18, *the gates of hell shall not prevail against it*," Lincoln suggests that the political order must contend against the same forces of sin and death that have characterized the human situation since the fall of mankind. The new pillars of intelligence, morality, and constitutional reverence, "hewn from the solid quarry of sober reason," are the political analogue to the rock of Peter.

FOUNDING, PERPETUATION, AND SALVATION

In many of his pre-presidential speeches, Lincoln found occasion to praise Washington, usually but not always in the final paragraphs. In the Lyceum Address, that praise is religiously inflected, in keeping with the call for a political religion of reverential obedience. In the Temperance Address, his paean to Washington involves a natural rather than supernatural referent, but it is just as lavish. The name of Washington, in its "naked deathless splendor," is compared to the brightness of the sun, which no encomium could increase. A few years later, in his prosecutorial attack on Polk's Mexican-American War, Congressman Lincoln demands that the "bewildered, confounded, and miserably-perplexed man" answer his interrogatories: "Let him remember he sits where Washington sat; and, so remembering, let him answer as Washington would answer." In more tempered rhetoric, the speeches at both Peoria and Cooper Union mention Washington in their perorations, highlighting the nation's betrayal of "such a chief as Washington," through the sophistry of "invocations to Washington, imploring men to unsay what Washington said, and undo what Washington did." This regular element of Lincoln's rhetoric disappears from his presidential speeches. Significantly, Lincoln's last explicit appeal to the legacy of Washington comes in his Springfield Farewell, as he departs for the White House, "with," he says, "a task before me greater than that which rested upon Washington." That greater task of perpetuating the Union by saving the Union leads Lincoln to allude to "the assistance of that Divine Being who ever attended him," hoping that his neighbors will commend him to "His care." Lincoln's turn to the highest authority, or more accurately his turning of his audience toward the highest authority—no longer as an analogue or point of comparison or background assumption, but directly—can be seen in his First Inaugural and nearly every other major presidential speech. In the place where we might have expected the invocation of Washington, Lincoln instead recommends "a firm reliance on Him, who has never yet forsaken this favored land." Bigger guns than Washington will be required to meet the crisis of the Civil War.

2

The Gettysburg Address

1776 and Devotion to the Declaration

The Gettysburg Address has become *the* most famous American speech. In fact, it makes the Top Ten list of speeches in any language. It's right up there with the Apology of Socrates and the Funeral Oration of Pericles, with the added benefit that Lincoln's was actually written and delivered by him, whereas the speeches by Socrates and Pericles come to us second-hand, with the editorial assistance of Plato and Thucydides. Phrases from the Gettysburg Address crop up all over; article 2 of the current French Constitution states that the principle of the republic is *"gouvernment du peuple, par le peuple et pour le peuple."* American politicians pay homage to Lincoln's formulations by borrowing shamelessly from him, sometimes with attribution, sometimes not.

This familiarity poses certain problems. Because the Lyceum Address was a lesser-known Lincoln production, we had the benefit of being able to approach it with fewer preconceptions. With a text we believe we know, the temptation to skip steps and push to the "takeaway" is strong. Resisting that impulse will require patience. Of course, previous acquaintance is not all bad. If you received a good education (or at least an old-fashioned one), you might be able to recite the Gettysburg Address from memory. If you can, do so now. If you cannot, then read through it half a dozen times.

Four score and seven years ago our fathers brought forth on this continent, a new nation, conceived in Liberty, and dedicated to the proposition that all men are created equal.

Now we are engaged in a great civil war, testing whether that nation, or any nation so conceived and so dedicated, can long endure. We are met on a great battle-field of that war. We have come to dedicate a portion of that field, as a final resting place for those who here gave their lives that that nation might live. It is altogether fitting and proper that we should do this.

But, in a larger sense, we can not dedicate—we can not consecrate—we can not hallow—this ground. The brave men, living and dead, who struggled here, have consecrated it, far above our poor power to add or detract. The world will little note, nor long remember what we say here, but it can never forget what they did here. It is for us the living, rather, to be dedicated here to the unfinished work which they who fought here have thus far so nobly advanced. It is rather for us to be here

> dedicated to the great task remaining before us—that
> from these honored dead we take increased devotion to
> that cause for which they gave the last full measure of
> devotion—that we here highly resolve that these dead
> shall not have died in vain—that this nation, under God,
> shall have a new birth of freedom—and that government
> of the people, by the people, for the people, shall not
> perish from the earth.

In the interest of restoring naiveté, we might start by raising a doubt about an interpretive leap that students commonly make. With satisfaction, they note the irony of Lincoln's claim that "The world will little note, nor long remember what we say here, but it can never forget what they did here." Young people love irony; spotting it lifts one into the ranks of the cognoscenti. And this instance seems such easy pickings. Most believe the irony was intentional; in other words, the irony is not simply a precipitate of history (the disproportion between the actual result and Lincoln's stated expectation) but rather his premeditated underselling of his speech, and of speech itself in relation to deeds. That may be; in due course we will need to consider what is being said about the relation between speech and deed. However, the ready assumption of irony can preempt a fuller inquiry. The surface may be more complex than is suggested by the notion of false modesty.

For one thing, to assume false modesty on Lincoln's part requires that the "we" of "what we say here" is the royal we—a stand-in for "I." Yet it would be odd to use the majestic plural in a supposedly self-effacing statement. Moreover, Lincoln is strict about his pronouns; the practice of using "we" to refer to oneself, known as nosism, is not one of his rhetorical devices. Posing even more of a problem for this suggestion is that "we" and its affiliates "our" and "us" are used repeatedly in the Gettysburg Address. There are ten instances of "we," three of "us," two of "our," and not a single use of "I." In every case, the reference is genuinely to the collective, those who gathered together to dedicate the cemetery at Gettysburg, Pennsylvania, and, by extension, all loyal, "living" Unionists. Remember, too, that by the time Lincoln took to the podium to deliver his brief concluding remarks, the event was in its third hour of continuous speech. In point of fact, Lincoln was correct about the world's not remembering what was said that day. The main event on November 19, 1863, was not Lincoln's two-minute dedication but Edward Everett's two-hour oration entitled "The Battles of Gettysburg." Very few Americans since have bothered to read it. It's not a bad speech. Everett, after all, was a Harvard-educated president of Harvard, reputed to be the finest orator of his day, the successor to Old Man Eloquent himself, Daniel Webster. Nonetheless, Everett's performance is remembered only because his intense and lengthy effort was so thoroughly outshone by Lincoln's little squib. It is also the case that, without the ultimate victory of the Union cause, the remarks even of Lincoln might have been forgotten. Although there were prescient appreciators of the speech at the time, it took many decades for it to ascend to its canonical position in American memory.

But *noting* and *remembering* are not enough. We want to *understand*. What did Lincoln accomplish and how did he do it? Maybe especially, how did he do what he did in such brief compass? As Everett graciously acknowledged, "I should be glad, if I could flatter myself, that I came as near to the central idea of the occasion in two hours, as you did in two minutes." The Gettysburg Address contains 3 paragraphs, 10 sentences, and 271 words (word counts vary slightly depending on the version of the text and whether "four score," "can not" and "battle-field" are formatted as one or two words). Astonishingly, since many words are used more than once, the speech is comprised of only half that number of distinct words, the great majority of them single-syllabled. Lincoln might have excelled at writing sound-bites and tweets. The contrast with Everett was dramatic: just in the first two of Everett's 58 paragraphs, there are a baker's dozen of four-syllable words (like "funereal" and "lamentations") and dozens more with three syllables (like "obsequies" and "interment"). Everett luxuriates in his latinate vocabulary. His lengthy procemium is an erudite account of Athenian burial practices. Following upon the Harvardian's classicizing indulgence, Lincoln's plain style is almost a rebuke, even without the speech's plea for more action, less talk.

FROM JULY TO NOVEMBER

Before delving into Lincoln's few words, it might help to situate the occasion. The battle of Gettysburg took place at the beginning of July 1863. It was a Union victory, with the Confederates fleeing the field on July 4th, and in retrospect we know that it was a turning point of the war, though that was not so evident at the time. The casualties were like those of so many Civil War battles, staggering belief—51,000 American dead and wounded in three days. To gain a sense of the scale of the carnage, contrast it with more familiar numbers, like the 58,000 American soldiers who died during our twenty-year involvement in Vietnam or the 7,000 from the War on Terror, now also in its twentieth year. Remember that the population then was one-tenth what it is now. Translating the death toll from the Civil War into the nation's current population would mean 7.5 million dead.

Democratic peoples, being peace-loving, tend to tire of war, to quail before its terrible blood price. Politically, Lincoln was confronting this problem of war-weariness, the way in which grief saps morale and commitment. The problem was not limited to the passivity or hopelessness of grief. There was active resistance to the continuance of the war. In the immediate wake of the victory at Gettysburg, riots over the draft broke out in New York City. Over four days, in the middle of that July, 120 civilians were killed, including 11 Black citizens who were lynched by angry mobs; hundreds of Blacks fled the city; upwards of 2,000 people were injured; and 50 buildings burned to the ground. It took the arrival of thousands of federal troops, who were diverted from their pursuit of Lee's Confederate army and marched instead 200 miles north, to restore order. Some said the New York draft riots turned a Union victory into a Confederate one.

The Gettysburg Address is emphatically a war speech—a speech designed to rally the nation to stay the course. Students, not knowing much history, but aware that Lincoln is beloved for his kindliness and his summons to bind up the nation's wounds, often miss the martial implications of the speech. Just as they overlay the eventual fame of the Gettysburg Address onto the original, they overlay the charity of the Second Inaugural onto it. They assume that Lincoln is commemorating all the fallen— and they appreciate his supposed inclusiveness, especially in contrast to the bombast and arrogance of Pericles, whose Funeral Oration vaunts his city of Athens at the expense of the Spartan enemy.

Yet, perhaps this misreading might be excused, since a most unusual war speech it is. Lincoln never mentions the enemy, or rather he mentions them only by implication. When Lincoln speaks of "those who here gave their lives that that nation might live," his audience would have been acutely aware that there were others who gave their lives that that nation might die, that it might no longer be the United States. The burial ground at Gettysburg was exclusively for those who served the Union; the event was billed as "The Inauguration of the National Cemetery at Gettysburg." In the weeks before the dedication, the townspeople had witnessed the reinterment process, as thousands of the battle-dead were exhumed from the shallow graves in which they had hastily been placed by those same local citizens back in the sweltering days of July. As the bodies of the fallen were uncovered, the Union dead were painstakingly identified and separated from the Confederate dead. While the rebels were simply reburied, coffin-less, deeper in the ground where they were found (to be reclaimed later by their home states), the loyal dead were removed, further sorted into their military units, and placed in coffins, the coffins then arranged in orderly lines, awaiting proper burial in the new cemetery.

Lincoln's remarks apply only to these "honored dead." Even so, he is careful to preserve the conditions for restored communion with those whom he once addressed as "my dissatisfied fellow countrymen" (First Inaugural). The rhetorical constraints on marshalling commitment to fight a civil war are very different from the free-wheeling license possible during foreign war—just take a look at George S. Patton, Jr.'s Speech to the Third Army, among whose many unforgettable obscenities is this sequence: "We're not going to just shoot the sons-of-bitches, we're going to rip out their living Goddamned guts and use them to grease the treads of our tanks. We're going to murder those lousy Hun cocksuckers by the bushel-fucking-basket." The language used by "Old Blood and Guts" Patton is quite literally visceral. Lincoln, by contrast, searches for a way to rally the nation while abjuring such characterizations. He refuses either to demonize or dehumanize. Of course, not all in the north refrained from bad-mouthing Johnny Reb, and certainly Confederate excoriation of the "Damn Yankees" seldom observed any rhetorical rules of engagement.

This observation about Lincoln's abstraction from the enemy leads to a general observation about the highly abstract character of the entire speech. No specifics are given. There isn't a proper noun to be found, with the single exception of God. Thus, there is no mention of Gettysburg, just "a great battlefield." There is no mention of America, just "this continent." There is no mention of the United States, just "a new nation" and "that nation" and "this nation." There is no mention of the parties to the conflict, no North or South, no Union or Confederacy, just "a great civil war." Lincoln speaks of "our fathers," but no names are given. And although the opening clause, "Four score and seven years ago," does refer to a specific date, if one had no knowledge of when the speech was delivered, the precise referent would be lost, lodged somewhere long ago. The tremendous abstraction or generality of the speech is part of what explains the ability of the Gettysburg Address to speak to people in different eras and cultures who have no connection to the events of that day and who yet feel, as Lincoln might say, "as though they were blood of the blood, and flesh of the flesh" of those spoken of there.

The abstraction of the Gettysburg Address is in marked contrast to the impromptu speech that Lincoln had given on July 7th, right after the victory, when residents of the District of Columbia assembled outside the White House (unimpeded by barricades) to serenade him. In these extemporaneous remarks, Lincoln prefigures points he will make in November. However, he does so in very different language, informal and highly specific. After thanking the visitors, he says:

> How long ago is it—eighty odd years—since on the Fourth of July for the first time in the history of the world a nation by its representatives, assembled and declared as a self-evident truth that "all men are created equal." That was the birthday of the United States of America.

After mentioning by name Thomas Jefferson and John Adams, and the providential fact of their joint deaths on the fiftieth anniversary of the Declaration, Lincoln goes on to describe the significance of the victory at Gettysburg:

> and now, on this last Fourth of July just passed, when we have a gigantic Rebellion, at the bottom of which is an effort to overthrow the principle that all men are created equal, we have the surrender of a most powerful position and army on that very day, and not only so, but in a succession of battles in Pennsylvania, near to us, through three days, so rapidly fought that they might be called one great battle on the 1st,

2d, and 3d of the month of July; and on the 4th the cohorts of those who opposed the declaration that all men are created equal, "turned tail" and ran. Gentlemen, this is a glorious theme, and the occasion for a speech, but I am not prepared to make one worthy of the occasion.

Four months later, he was ready. The improvised materials had undergone a kind of sublimation.

THE ORIGINS

The first paragraph consists of only one sentence. It describes the past, the nation's beginnings. Writers make choices; careful writers weigh those choices. In his 1852 eulogy of Henry Clay, Lincoln had begun,

On the fourth day of July, 1776, the people of a few feeble and oppressed colonies of Great Britain, inhabiting a portion of the Atlantic coast of North America, publicly declared their national independence, and made their appeal to the justice of their cause, and to the God of battles, for the maintainance of that declaration.

In the decade following, he shifted from directly naming the nation's birthdate to a refracted mode of reference that instead emphasized the passage of time. So, for instance, at Peoria in 1854, Lincoln said, "**Near eighty years ago** we began by declaring that all men are created equal." At Kalamazoo in 1856, he said, "We are **eighty years old**." A year later, in the *Dred Scott* speech, he offered this parody of Douglas's butchery of the Declaration: "'We hold these truths to be self-evident that all British subjects who were on this continent **eighty-one years ago**, were created equal to all British subjects born and *then* residing in Great Britain.'" At Chicago a year later, he spoke repeatedly of the nation's having "endured **eighty-two years**" and, in a discussion of the purposes of "these 4th of July gatherings," described how "we run our memory back over the pages of history for **about eighty-two years**." Finally, in the serenade speech just days after the battle of Gettysburg, he spoke of the nation's "**eighty odd years**."

Why did he not continue his confirmed practice and begin the Gettysburg Address by saying "Eighty-seven years ago"? Why this substitute: "Four score and seven years ago"? Mathematically, of course, the two formulations are equivalent. Yet, he made his audience and all subsequent readers do a fair bit of arithmetic in order to puzzle out the date. For those not familiar with old English terms of measurement—like a bushel and a peck, or an ell and a dram—a "score" is a period of twenty years. "Four score" (four times twenty) "and seven" (plus seven) equals eighty-seven years. The address was delivered in 1863; subtracting eighty-seven from 1863 takes you back to 1776. Note that either formulation ("eighty-seven" or "four score and seven") requires knowledge of the date of the speech's delivery. Thus, it is not just 1776 that is commemorated. 1863 is enshrined forever as the minuend (the mathematical term for the part you start with before you take away the subtrahend). It is often said that Lincoln must have chosen his opening phrase because it sounded more poetic than the alternatives, but I must say it is an odd form of poetry that requires multiplication, addition, and subtraction. By the time the audience had performed the three operations to arrive at 1776, the speech would have been over.

The phrase "four score and seven" does, of course, evoke the beautiful language and cadence of the King James Bible. Lincoln's audience would have been familiar with the Ninetieth Psalm, which numbered the human lifespan at "threescore and ten," or at most, "fourscore." Many of them would also have known that the reason given for why the life of man is so "soon cut off" is that we spend our days in "labor and sorrow," consumed by God's wrath. By thus alluding to Scripture's harsh verdict on the lifespan of sinners, Lincoln forces us to wonder whether there are similar limits on the lifespan of mankind's political collectives. The nation, at four score and seven, is now just beyond the furthest term of an individual life. Moreover, as the audience well knows, and Lincoln soon acknowledges, the nation is engaged in a terrible civil war—a war that might cause the nation to perish.

Before he even gets to any mention of the war, in this one-sentence opening paragraph, which seems to be a purely admiring description of the achievement of the founding fathers, Lincoln is able to strike a darker note—a note of inevitable and perhaps incipient death—through this phrase "four score and seven." In the ears of Americans, "1776" always has a hopeful and joyous ring to it; that year, though bygone, looks forward; it smiles on the future. By contrast, "four score and seven years ago" has a somber resonance, hinting at the passing away of "the days of our years." In the closing of his 1859 address at the Wisconsin state fair, Lincoln had indicated that this was the wisdom of the East as well: "It is said an Eastern monarch once charged his wise men to invent him a sentiment to be ever in view, and which should be true and appropriate in all times and situations. They presented him the words, 'And this, too, shall pass

away.'" So, yes, "four score and seven" is poetic, but not in the sense of a flowery fancying-up of ordinary speech; rather, like all genuine poetry, it imbues language with more complex and multilayered meanings—meanings that work upon and move the audience whether they are aware of it or not.

One final observation about the word "score." In its oldest denotation, it describes an activity that can be traced all the way back to the Paleolithic era, when numerical records were kept by scoring, which is to say cutting or notching, a piece of ivory, or bone, or wood. The scored item, sometimes called a tally stick, was a way of tracking the passage of time (or other quantities) that stretched beyond the verge of human memory. So, we might say that Lincoln begins the Gettysburg Address by presenting the nation's tally stick or scorecard.[1] Remember, he had done something similar in the second sentence of the Lyceum Address, although there the timeline was not the political one but the natural one of the earth's existence and the historical/religious one of Christianity. Because no member of his audience, at that moment in 1863, could have been a participant in the events of 1776, American citizens were in need of new, more permanent, less flesh-bound forms of remembrance. What Lincoln does in the first paragraph of the Gettysburg Address is carve a solid and enduring substitute. He condenses the meaning of the Declaration into one sentence. His formulation is lapidary—a sentence that can be scored into memory.

This sentence is a culmination of reflections on the Declaration that Lincoln had been intensively engaged in for the past decade. Speaking from Independence Hall in Philadelphia, on the birthday of George Washington, President-elect Lincoln made a striking claim. He said that he had "never had a feeling politically that did not spring from the sentiments embodied in the Declaration of Independence." Appeals to the Declaration are found not only in nearly every major speech but in letters and even scraps of paper on which Lincoln develops arguments possibly for future use. Sustained treatments of the Declaration can be found in his Peoria Address of 1854, his Kalamazoo Address of 1856, his speech on the *Dred Scott* decision in 1857, and then the great rush of speeches during the senatorial campaign against Stephen Douglas in 1858, including not only the seven Lincoln–Douglas debates, but also major speeches in Chicago and Springfield. In fact, the only major speeches during the decade of the 1850s that don't center on the Declaration are the House Divided speech and the address at Cooper Union. Because the House Divided speech was given at the Republican nominating convention, Lincoln did not need to convince his audience "to re-adopt the Declaration"—indeed, the maintenance of its principles was the first item in the Republican Party platforms of 1856 and 1860.[2] As for Cooper Union, it presents an exclusively Constitution-based argument, setting forth with lawyerly precision the constitutional status of federal control over slavery in the territories, based on exhaustive research into the voting records of the founding generation.

Fittingly, after delivering the Gettysburg Address, Lincoln makes no further statements about the Declaration. His exposition of the document had achieved its final form. Moreover, the dedication to "a new birth of freedom," with which the Gettysburg Address concludes, marks a decisive moment— the beginning we might say of a new scorecard, a card that has been scored with the blood sacrifice of "these honored dead." The scenes of the Civil War will rival in American memory the scenes of the Revolution, just as the sentences of Lincoln rival those of Jefferson.

As to what happened "four score and seven years ago," Lincoln presents an elaborate metaphor that refers to three distinct moments: conception, birth, and baptism. The moments, however, are presented out of their usual order. Missing are any references to representative assemblies or the protracted war for independence. Instead of attempting to recapture the spirited struggle of the revolutionary era, Lincoln substitutes more peaceful, natural imagery: "our fathers brought forth on this continent, a new nation." The nation's nativity is linked to a document rather than the historical drama. Speaking in Chicago in 1858, Lincoln had noted that the immigrant half of the population did not have the founders as their "fathers and grandfathers" and as a result, "If they look back through this history to trace their connection with those days by blood, they find they have none, they cannot carry themselves back into that glorious epoch and make themselves feel that they are part of us." Lincoln argues for a truer, and more expansive, form of belonging than that based on biology. When these later arrivals to America

look through that old Declaration of Independence, they find that those old men say that "We hold these truths to be self-evident, that all men are created equal," and then they feel that that moral sentiment taught in that day evidences their relation to those men, that it is the father of all moral principle in them, and that they have a right to claim it as though they were blood of the blood, and flesh of the flesh, of the men who wrote the declaration, and so they are.

Note that, at Gettysburg, although Lincoln acknowledges "this continent," he does not suggest that the nation emerges from out of the soil. Our founding is not like the old myths of autochthony where the people were said to spring forth from the earth, like the Spartoi of Thebes sown from the dragon's teeth. Our nation is "on" the continent, not "from" or "out of" it. This distinction between the land and the nation is present in the opening of the Lyceum Address also. There he credits the ancestors with having a double task: "to possess themselves . . . of this goodly land; and to uprear upon its hills and its valleys, a political edifice of liberty and equal rights." Land may be a prerequisite of nationhood, but ours is not a blood-and-soil patriotism. Our origins are instead ideational, based on declaratory words, which Lincoln in his fragment on "The Constitution and the Union" called both "a philosophical cause" and "*the* word, '*fitly spoken.*'" I disagree here with a number of commentators who argue that we have the founders for our fathers and the continent for our mother; they regard "brought forth on" as equivalent to begat or sired. However, "to bring forth" is another common biblical phrase that, from Genesis forward, refers to the female role of parturition, or in the case of plants, the visible appearance of fruit. There are even Bible verses that apply the obstetrical metaphor politically, describing the national destiny of Israel, as in Micah 4:10: "Be in pain, and labour to bring forth, O daughter of Zion, like a woman in travail: for now shalt thou go forth out of the city, and thou shalt dwell in the field, and thou shalt go *even* to Babylon; there shalt thou be delivered; there the LORD shall redeem thee from the hand of thine enemies." In the New Testament, the promise of redemption through birth is repeated and transfigured, as in Matthew 1:21: "And she shall bring forth a son, and thou shalt call his name JESUS: for he shall save his people from their sins." Accordingly, I suspect Lincoln of a bit of metaphorical gender-bending: our fathers are really our mothers, for they birthed a new nation.

Lincoln's next two clauses mention two key ideas, liberty and equality, each of which is linked to the dominant metaphor of birth. Casting back before the advent moment in 1776 to the moment of conception, Lincoln says the new nation was "conceived in Liberty." What could that mean? How literally should this language of sexual congress be taken? Of course, "to conceive" can denote either a physical or a mental phenomenon: becoming pregnant or taking a notion into the mind. Before the nation could be brought forth into practical realization, it had to be thought of or imagined. Whence arose the concept? According to Lincoln, it originated "in Liberty." Of the handful of common nouns that appear mid-sentence throughout the speech, this is the only one Lincoln capitalized, although he might have capitalized "people" (as he did in both the Lyceum and Temperance Addresses, as well as in some of his Thanksgiving Proclamations), or "freedom" (this being the proper name, so to speak, of the new birth prophesied at the end of the speech). The result is that "Liberty" and "God" are, in effect, the only capitalized words, since each of the others ("four," "now," "we" [twice], "it" [three times], "but," and "the" [twice]) would not be capitalized but for their sentence-starting position.

Why does Lincoln incarnate liberty in this way and what does it mean to be "conceived in Liberty"? Whenever a difficulty in interpreting Lincoln arises, the Bible is a good starting place. Psalm 51:5 speaks of being conceived in sin: "Behold, I was shapen in iniquity; and in sin did my mother conceive me"—a passage that takes one back to Genesis 3:16: "Unto the woman he said, I will greatly multiply thy sorrow and thy conception; in sorrow thou shalt bring forth children." Quite different is the Gospel description of the virgin birth. In Luke 1:31, the angel tells Mary, "And, behold, thou shalt conceive in thy womb, and bring forth a son," and in Matthew 1:20, the angel assures Joseph that "that which is conceived in her is of the Holy Ghost." According to Lincoln's redaction, the new nation was conceived not in sin or sorrow but in liberty, although given the use that humans make of their liberty, there might not be much difference between the two terms. Beneath the beautiful thought that the nation was conceived in the pure womb of liberty there lurks the afterthought—the afterthought evoked by the distant resonance of Psalm 51's "conceived in sin." Psalm 51, known as the *Miserere*, is the most famous of the seven penitential psalms. In it, a contrite King David prays for a clean heart and a renewed spirit after his unjust taking of Bathsheba, the wife of the humble Uriah. The old Adamic/Davidic conception in sin and the new salvific one in the womb of Mary are explicitly linked through the genealogy that opens the book of Matthew. The list of forty-one generations (the "begats") is interrupted only twice, once to interject that "David the king begat Solomon of her *that had been the wife* of Urias" and then to mention that fourteen generations later the Israelites were "carried away to Babylon." Among the wages of David's sin was civil war brought on by the insurrection of his son Absalom. (The parallels between the Biblical and American stories were explored by another of our literary giants, William Faulkner, in *Absalom, Absalom!*)

Lincoln, in his very frank 1855 letter to his dearest friend, Joshua Speed, uses a variant of "conceived in sin" when he declares that the Kansas-Nebraska Act "was conceived in violence, passed in violence, is maintained in violence, and is being executed in violence." Lincoln goes so far as to wish the fate of Haman (who plotted the genocide of the Jews but ended on a gallows of his own making) on those who try to deprive Blacks of their legal right to freedom in free territories.

While I believe that Lincoln's poetry is deep enough to sound these darker echoes of sin, sorrow, and violence, the surface meaning of "conceived in Liberty" seems altogether positive, although not perfectly clear. John Channing Briggs, a sensitive analyst of Lincoln's rhetoric, stresses the obscurity of Lincoln's phrasing: "Certainly, if one presses the metaphor to its sensible limit, the nation had parentage; but the manner and precise timing of its conception . . . is hidden as well as enacted in Liberty."[3] Leon Kass, in the last essay in his recent collection *Leading a Worthy Life,* has offered the most comprehensive attempt to plumb these mysteries. He uncovers three possibilities. Perhaps Lincoln means to suggest that, just as a child might be conceived in love, the nation was conceived in liberty. Liberty, or maybe love of liberty, was the seminal passion that eventually produced the nation. Or perhaps "conceived in Liberty" indicates that the idea of a new nation was freely formed and chosen. While the Declaration itself insists on the force of "necessity," Lincoln instead highlights the operation of free will; the nation was conceived in an act of liberty. One final possibility is that Lincoln means to refer further back, even centuries back, into the colonial period. Alexis de Tocqueville, for instance, argues that the spirit of liberty was present from the first in the English colonies. He explains how the aristocratic liberty of the mother country assumed a new, more democratic form in the New World. If so, then British liberty was the womb (the Latin is *matrix*) within which the new nation gestated. These three speculations are not incompatible with one another: a love of liberty, long present among the colonists, did flare up in one decisive, freely chosen act, transforming British subjects into founders.

I have one further hunch about the organic, "gentle" character of Lincoln's account of the nation's origins. I suspect he didn't want to come anywhere near words like "revolution" or "independence" while in the midst of putting down "a gigantic Rebellion" (to use the blunt language of his off-the-cuff speech of July 7). For Lincoln, there is a crystal-clear distinction between a justified revolution, undertaken in response to well-documented violations of rights, and an unjustified rebellion in which one portion of a democratic people, unhappy with the results of a perfectly constitutional election, attempts to nullify that election by secession. The secessionists were in no way comparable to the American revolutionaries. However, Lincoln didn't have time in this speech to explain the theoretical difference, as he did at length in other speeches, especially his First Inaugural. Instead, he found euphemisms for the American Revolution like "brought forth" and "conceived in Liberty." He uses the language of generative congress to describe an act of political separation. Given that he was resisting those who wanted a further separation, it was not the time to praise the dissolution of political bands.

After liberty, the other feature of the founding that is highlighted is equality. Lincoln says the nation is "dedicated to the proposition that all men are created equal." Whereas liberty is linked backward to the nation's conception, equality is more prospective; it involves dedication. As in the moment of christening or baptism, the infant nation is placed on a certain path by its progenitors. Although Lincoln quotes (accurately) from the Declaration, he puts his own gloss on it, famously introducing some key changes.

As we all either know or should know, the Declaration speaks of equality as a truth held to be "self-evident" by the American people. They knew that this self-evident truth was unfortunately not evident to everyone the world over, but they expected that, in time, the scales would fall from the eyes of others (temporarily blinded by false teachings, such as that about the divine right of kings). "Self-evident" is a term borrowed from geometry. A self-evident truth is an axiom. An axiom doesn't require proof and, in fact, it cannot be proved. You either see it or you don't. If $a = b$ and $b = c$, then $a = c$. According to the Declaration, human equality is like that; it is axiomatic. All men—black and white, male and female—simply are equal in the relevant sense of being endowed by their creator with natural rights to life and liberty. This is the essential truth of the human condition. This foundational truth is not invalidated by the harsh fact that most human beings, in most times and places, have lived under political orders that violate their natural rights, slavery being the most dramatic instance. According to the Declaration, despotic regimes and unjust institutions are illegitimate. It follows that people may exercise their right of revolution in order to establish new governments founded upon the consent of the governed and respectful of the individuals' pre-existing natural rights.

Although there are plenty of places where Lincoln uses the orthodox language of "axiom" or "self-evident" to describe the primary, capital-T truths of the Declaration, his most famous

formulation, here in the Gettysburg Address, calls human equality a "proposition." "Proposition" is another term borrowed
from geometry. Unlike an axiom, a proposition requires a proof.
That's why one must be "dedicated" to it. It's a theorem that
must be demonstrated in practice. That Lincoln was well aware
of the distinction between axioms and propositions is evident
from his Letter to H. L. Pierce in 1859, where he says:

> One would start with great confidence that he could con-
> vince any sane child that the simpler propositions of Euclid
> are true; but, nevertheless, he would fail, utterly, with one
> who should deny the definitions and axioms. The principles
> of Jefferson are the definitions and axioms of free society.

What might explain Lincoln's shift from one Euclidean term
to the other? Does Lincoln suddenly doubt the truth of human
equality? Not at all. It's rather that he wants to highlight the
needfulness of translating an abstract truth into concrete political form. As early as the Lyceum Address, Lincoln described
the founders as experimental scientists or mathematicians drawn
to an unproven proposition. "Their ambition," he said, "aspired
to display before an admiring world, a practical demonstration
of the truth of a proposition, which had hitherto been considered, at best no better, than problematical; namely, *the capability of a people to govern themselves*." In that formulation, it was
self-government—the corollary of equality—that needed to be
proved. The current crisis, however, was more severe. At the
time of the founding, there was general agreement that all were
created equal, even if there was no political ability on the part
of the very weak federal government to do much about the do-

mestic institution of slavery in the states. Nonetheless, all then understood that slavery was an evil; even those who argued that slavery was necessary, and there were many of those, had the decency to call it "a necessary evil." But subsequent generations had fallen away from this view. Led by John C. Calhoun, southerners had taken to openly repudiating the truths of the Declaration, calling equality "a self-evident lie" and slavery "a positive good." The heresy was not limited to southerners; John Pettit of Indiana had coined the catch-phrase "a self-evident lie," as Lincoln disdainfully noted.

In the 1850s, as the crisis of the "house divided" escalated, Lincoln argued that the crisis had arisen because a substantial portion of the American people had let go of the truth on which their own rights depended. Lincoln put it concisely in his 1854 Peoria Address: "When the white man governs himself that is self-government; but when he governs himself, and also governs *another* man, that is *more* than self-government—that is despotism." Since the Civil War was brought on by a serious departure from the meaning of both equality and consent, it seems right for Lincoln, when speaking in the midst of that war, to imply that a truth once firmly held as self-evident had now moved into the ranks of a propositional truth that must be proved in action—that action being the restoration of a Union dedicated to the principle of equality. We see here that the language of mathematics might not be perfectly suited to (or congruent with) politics, since political truths depend on being held in the heart as true. The Declaration, after all, did not say that the truths were self-evident but rather that "we hold" them to be so. To firm up our loosening grip, the Gettysburg Address superimposes religious language ("dedicate," "consecrate," "hallow") on its Euclidean substrate.

In his opening paragraph, in thirty words, Lincoln has performed an act of remembrance. His description of "our fathers" is meant to make his audience reverential. But, at the same time, the generative imagery conveys the message that each successive cohort of Americans is essential to the maturation or completion of the founding. The needed proof is ongoing. It is up to us to live out the timeless truth to which the nation has been pledged. With this single sentence, Lincoln forms the nation's self-understanding, uniting filial piety with progress. Action here and now is mandated by fidelity to the past. Lincoln's political stance manages to combine liberal elements with profoundly conservative elements.

THE STRUGGLE

The gloss Lincoln puts on the Declaration of Independence leads directly to the next paragraph, and its opening word: "Now." This paragraph, more than twice the length of the first (four sentences, seventy-two words), explains the meaning of the "great civil war." The war is a "test," and what is being tested is "whether that nation, or any nation so conceived and so dedicated, can long endure." Curiously, Lincoln does not say "our nation"; he says "that nation"—in other words, the one described above in the opening paragraph. He doesn't want the audience to stray outside the bounds of the idea he so carefully shaped there. What is at stake is the survival of that new nation that sought to combine liberty and equality. And more than that: at stake is the very possibility of political life based on such premises. Lincoln enlarges the stakes beyond national survival. The failure of the American experiment would constitute the failure of popular government altogether.

This assertion of American exceptionalism may sound in-flated or hyperbolic, but I think it emerges more from humility than hubris. What makes the American case so special, so exem-plary? The answer was best formulated by General Washington in his 1783 Circular to the States, his first valedictory, offering counsel to the nation upon the conclusion of the Revolutionary War. There he described our privileged situation, the confluence of factors that gifted us with "a fairer opportunity for political happiness, than any other Nation has ever been favored with" (enviable geography plus the Enlightenment package of rights, literacy, commerce, and moderate religion). Today, individuals are advised to "check your privilege"—despite the often grating sanctimony of the injunction, awareness of how much one's sit-uation is attributable to good fortune is part of self-knowledge. So, too, with American greatness. Washington "called out" American privilege to deliver a stern verdict: "if their Citizens should not be completely free and happy, the fault will be in-tirely [sic] their own." Lincoln's point is the same. If popular government is not sustainable in the United States, favored as it is, then what are the probabilities in less advantaged places?

It is striking how similar the language of the Gettysburg Ad-dress is to the language of Lincoln's 1861 Message to Congress in Special Session. Claiming that "this issue embraces more than the fate of these United States," Lincoln explains the stakes of the conflict then just beginning:

It presents to the whole family of man the question, whether a constitutional republic, or democracy—a Government of the people by the same people—can or cannot maintain its territorial integrity against its own domestic foes. It presents the question, whether discontented individuals . . . can . . . break up their Government, and thus practically put an end to free government upon the earth.

The lawbreaking against which Lincoln warned in the Lyceum Address had reached a suicidal pitch. Under threat was the very essence of popular government: free elections. Later in the address, Lincoln expands on what will be required if the people are to pass the test, which is one of *maintenance* rather than establishment:

It is now for them to demonstrate to the world that those who can fairly carry an election can also suppress a rebellion; that ballots are the rightful and peaceful successors of bullets; and that when ballots have fairly and constitutionally decided, there can be no successful appeal back to bullets; that there can be no successful appeal except to ballots themselves, at succeeding elections. Such will be a great lesson of peace; teaching men that what they cannot take by an election, neither can they take by a war; teaching all the folly of being the beginners of a war.

These lengthier passages, addressed to Congress in the first months of the war, help to explicate the more condensed, poetic rendering at Gettysburg, where Lincoln, communing with a grieving public, conveyed the purpose of the war. Paradoxically or not, this "great lesson of peace" must be midwifed by the war-power of the government.

As Lincoln understood, there was a perverse logic that led

from the theoretical denial of equality, as expressed in the South's schismatic view that slavery was "a positive good," to the denial of majority rule, as expressed in the South's attempted secession. The Declaration's truths are intertwined. Deny one and the others crumble, too. Lincoln's clearest statement of the illogic of secession appears in the First Inaugural, as the conclusion of the impressive train of reasoning dissecting the various theoretical and historical elements of the secessionist position.

Plainly, the central idea of secession, is the essence of anarchy. A majority, held in restraint by constitutional checks and limitations, and always changing easily with deliberate changes of popular opinions and sentiments is the only true sovereign of a free people. Whoever rejects it, does, of necessity, fly to anarchy or to despotism. Unanimity is impossible; the rule of a minority, as a permanent arrangement, is wholly inadmissible; so that, rejecting the majority principle, anarchy or despotism in some form is all that is left.

The dynamic of despotism was such that the rejection of first principles led inexorably to an assault not only on majority rule but on other constitutional rights as well. Since the mid-1830s, the new breed of advocates for slavery had sought to undermine the rights of speech, press, assembly, and petition—that is, whenever they were exercised by the opponents of slavery. Extensive censorship of the southern mails, undertaken in response to the abolitionists' postal campaign of 1835, followed by the "gag rule" first passed in 1836, forbidding the House of Representatives from hearing anti-slavery petitions, were the precursors to more far-reaching attempts to regulate "hate speech." One suspects that today's speech restrictionists—and they are growing in number—are unaware of the pro-slavery genealogy of their tactics. Frederick Douglass, always a defender of free speech, offered a graphic image of the policy in his 1854 response to the Kansas-Nebraska bill: "I understand the first purpose of the slave power to be the suppression of all antislavery discussion. . . . One end of the slave's chain must be fastened to a padlock in the lips of Northern freemen, else the slave will himself become free." Lincoln picked up this theme when, at the close of his Cooper Union Address, he wondered what, precisely, would "satisfy" the South. His conclusion: "This, and this only: cease to call slavery *wrong*, and join them in calling it *right*." The real demand of the South, in other words, was to silence the moral sense of the nation—a silencing that Lincoln had resisted since his 1837 Protest of the Illinois anti-abolition resolutions.

One is reminded of Martin Luther King, Jr.'s trenchant rendition: "injustice anywhere is a threat to justice everywhere." Aware of this linkage—aware of the inescapable reciprocity of rights—Lincoln always insisted that it was imperative to restore the belief in universal human equality for the sake of white citizens, as well as for the sake of the enslaved people. As he said in his 1862 State of the Union Address, in which he urged a constitutional amendment committing the nation to the abolition of slavery: "In *giving* freedom to the *slave*, we *assure* freedom to the *free*—honorable alike in what we give, and what we preserve." There are self-interested reasons to care for justice and these we should be glad to discover and exploit, since moral argument has a hard enough upstream journey as it is. Lincoln always de-spised the debased version of self-interest that utterly stripped away the moral contents of life—hence his hatred of the other Douglas's show of indifference toward slavery since it entailed "criticizing the Declaration of Independence, and insisting that there is no right principle of action but *self-interest*." At the same time, he always sought to educate and elevate self-interest by putting it in the same dinghy as justice, forcing them to row for shore together.

The primary purpose of the second paragraph of the Get-tysburg Address is to explain the stakes of the war. Its second-ary purpose is to comply with the organizer's request that "after the Oration, You, as Chief Executive of the Nation, formally set apart these grounds to their Sacred use by a few appropriate remarks." Lincoln performs his assignment, but in a most un-usual way, since he goes to some lengths not to utter the word "cemetery," instead saying they have assembled "to dedicate a portion of that field, as a final resting place for those who here gave their lives that that nation might live." This is his second reference to "that nation" rather than "our nation." Even at the risk of the awkwardness of "that that nation," Lincoln sticks with his insistence on reminding the audience of the antecedent paragraph where he defined the character of the new nation. This long euphemism, which stresses life (both the lives of the soldiers and the life of the nation) more than death (those who gave their lives are "resting"), is replaced by the pronoun "this" in the subsequent sentence: "It is altogether fitting and proper that we should do **this**," which is to say, "to dedicate a portion of that field, as a final resting place for those who here gave their lives that that nation might live." He writes a long version and a short version but in neither one does he use the word "cemetery." The very different, grief-drenched atmosphere of Edward Everett's address can be felt in the words chosen by the keynote speaker: "graves," "obsequies," "bones," "interment," "coffins," "remains," "deceased," "entombed," "monumental tumulus," "mound," "the Cemetery which we consecrate this day," and "sepulcher." Garry Wills, in his well-known book *Lincoln at Gettysburg*, argued that Lincoln, like Everett, was part of the romantic rural cemetery movement. I would incline to read the Gettysburg Address as more corrective than illustrative of the transcendentalist "culture of death."

More even than his diction, Lincoln's syntax reveals his unelegiac intentions. Although not classically schooled, indeed barely schooled at all, Lincoln made himself a master of what used to be called the Trivium: the three sequential studies of grammar, logic, and rhetoric. Since these were conceived as interlocking pathways to truth, an excursion through Lincoln's grammar can elucidate the logic of his argument and thereby help us understand the lasting rhetorical power of the Gettysburg Address. So, bear with me while I take you back to stuff you learned, or neglected to learn, in fifth grade.

Although an indifferent speller, Lincoln was a fine grammarian. Spelling, especially in English, is an erratic and unpredictable affair, but grammar is the bone and muscle of language. Lincoln taught himself the rudiments through such texts as Thomas Dilworth's *A New Guide to the English Tongue*. Every sentence must have a subject (even if bloggers today think it is catchy to write non-sentences). The chart below lists the ten subjects of the address's ten sentences.

Paragraph 1	sentence 1 (30 words)	**Our fathers**
Paragraph 2	sentence 2 (24 words)	**We**
	sentence 3 (10 words)	**We**
	sentence 4 (27 words)	**We**
	sentence 5 (11 words)	**It**
Paragraph 3	sentence 6 (19 words)	**We**
	sentence 7 (21 words)	**The brave men**
	sentence 8 (21 words)	**The world**
	sentence 9 (26 words)	**It**
	sentence 10 (82 words)	**It**

The one sentence of the first paragraph deals with **our fathers** and the nation they brought into being. The second paragraph moves from the past to the present moment, "Now," and makes three factual statements about what the new subject, the current generation, is doing: "**we** are engaged in a great civil war"; "**we** are met on a great battle-field of that war"; "**we** have come to dedicate a portion of that field." These three sentences are straightforward in their reliance on the simple subject "we." The fathers were generative, they were the beginning; we, by contrast, are in the midst of things, caught up in a great motion, embroiled, engaged, struggling to endure, but taking time out to provide a resting place for those no longer in the fight. Whereas the dedication spoken of in the first paragraph is prospective and propositional, the dedication of the second paragraph is retrospective and rooted. The cemetery at Gettysburg looks back in tribute to the fallen.

The last sentence of the second paragraph is very different

from the preceding sentences, for it expresses a judgment: "It is altogether fitting and proper that we should do this." That judgment is highlighted by a unique grammatical feature. "**It**" is the subject of the sentence, but what does "it" refer to? In apposition to "it" is the noun clause "that we should do this." Lincoln could have spoken more directly, dropping "it" and putting the noun clause first: "That we should do this is altogether fitting and proper." Lincoln chose a more complex syntax. This placement of "it" at the start of a sentence is called "anticipatory it" or "dummy it"—since the "it" anticipates the actual subject, which is deferred, only to be revealed later in the sentence. Interestingly, the effect of this syntactical transposition is to shift the natural stress of the sentence from the subject to the words that immediately follow the verb, in this case the phrase "altogether fitting and proper," and especially the word "altogether." "Fitting" and "proper" are predicate adjectives modified by the adverb "altogether," which describes just how fitting and proper our doing this is. By virtue of its peculiar structure, the sentence draws our attention not to the action so much as Lincoln's evaluation of the action. His verdict on the dedication of the cemetery is that it is "altogether fitting and proper"—not just "fitting," not just "proper," not just "fitting and proper," but "**altogether** fitting and proper."

Why did Lincoln want the word "altogether" to be the focal point of the sentence? I suspect he was sensitive to more than its literal, denotative meaning of "completely"; he was interested in its resonant power. Those who gave their lives for the life of the nation share this ground **together**, and we, by honoring them, are bound **together** with them. We are **all together**. The adverb "altogether" and the phrase "all together" are homophones. Lincoln makes no direct reference to the Union in this speech, but through syntax and word choice he creates a kind of telegraphic vibration: "**we**," "**we**," "**we**," "**altogether**."

THE PIVOT

In the second paragraph of the Gettysburg Address, Lincoln homes in on the present moment. The purpose for which they have gathered, "now" and "here," is the dedication of a cemetery to those who upheld the nation's dedication to equality. Given that Edward Everett had already delivered his lengthy oration, Lincoln might have been expected at this point to say something in his praise—something along the lines of "and our wonderful speaker has beautifully performed this task of dedication." Instead, Lincoln takes a very different tack. He says "It is altogether fitting and proper that we should do this . . . **But** . . ." Strict grammarians warn against starting sentences with "but"; how much more shocking to start a paragraph this way. Of course, the sticklers have their reasons; because "but" is a coordinating conjunction, it should be used to join parts of a sentence. If one were to diagram Lincoln's sentence, the "But" would be suspended in air on a dashed line pointing back to the previous sentence. Either Lincoln hadn't learned this lesson or perhaps his independent reading of the Bible—such as the Sermon on the Mount's repeated "But I say unto you . . ."—had taught him to ignore this purported rule. I am convinced that Lincoln's "But" is the most significant use of the word in the literature of English-speaking peoples. It is daring in more than a grammatical sense. Resorting to the adversative conjunctive always indicates that the speaker is seriously qualifying what he

has just said: if you hear "I love you, but . . ." you know something not good is coming: "I love you, but . . . I can't marry you."

What is Lincoln retracting in this third paragraph, a paragraph that is half again as long as the first two put together (5
sentences, 169 words)? He tells the audience they cannot do what
they came to do. He tells them bluntly and repeatedly, echoing
the three instances of "we" in the second paragraph with three
more, compressed into one sentence: "we can not dedicate—we
can not consecrate—we can not hallow—this ground." The
language and rituals of lamentation are inadequate to the task.
Lincoln pivots from words to deeds, insisting that the real consecration has already occurred. The "brave men" have already
accomplished it. Their struggle carries its own consecration.

Interestingly, Lincoln deviates from the usual meaning of the
word "consecrate," which in religious thought and practice does
involve speech. The best-known rite of consecration, among a
Christian people, would be Holy Communion, when a priest
or minister voices the "Words of Institution," based on 1st Corinthians 12:24–25, "Take, eat: this is my body, which is broken
for you: this do in remembrance of me. . . . This cup is the new
testament in my blood: this do ye, as oft as ye drink *it*, in remembrance of me." These words are more than evocative; they are
believed efficacious, with power to transform bread and wine
into body and blood. Although borrowing these terms "consecrate" and "hallow," Lincoln repurposes them. According to
him, speech is a "poor power" that can at best only "add" or "detract"; in other words, it cannot transubstantiate. These rituals
of remembrance, while "fitting and proper," do nothing to win
the war. The problem can be seen in the following paragraph
from Edward Everett's oration:

We have assembled, friends, fellow-citizens, at the invitation of the Executive of the great central State of Pennsylvania, seconded by the Governors of seventeen other loyal States of the Union, to pay the last tribute of respect to the brave men who, in the hard-fought battles of the first, second, and third days of July last, laid down their lives for the country on these hillsides and the plains before us, and whose remains have been gathered into the cemetery which we consecrate this day. As my eye ranges over the fields whose sods were so lately moistened by the blood of gallant and loyal men, I feel, as never before, how truly it was said of old that it is sweet and becoming to die for one's country. I feel, as never before, how justly, from the dawn of history to the present time, men have paid the homage of their gratitude and admiration to the memory of those who nobly sacrifice their lives, that their fellow-men may live in safety and in honor. And if this tribute were ever due, to whom could it be more justly paid than to those whose last resting-place we this day commend to the blessing of Heaven and of men?

Politically speaking, Everett's academic liturgy makes every mistake that could be made. He highlights the national division with his reference to eighteen loyal states; he endows the country with a physical existence but no moral content; he dwells on and romanticizes death in battle with that old chestnut *dulce et decorum est pro patria mori*; he very nearly implies that the war is over ("their fellow-men may live in safety"); and he leaves the living abandoned to the consolations of misty-eyed grief.

By contrast, Lincoln speaks for practical effect. His brevity accords with his negative verdict on purely eulogistic speech.[4]

Just as he re-labeled the truth of equality a "proposition" so that we might rise to the test of vindicating it, he ascends from "the ground" wherein the dead lie buried to "that cause" for which they died. What the Union soldiers advanced through their struggle and blood sacrifice, the living must see through to victory. Lincoln, like Pericles before him in his Funeral Oration, must redirect the energies of his audience to something more productive than mourning. He turns an elegy into a call to duty.

THE UNFINISHED WORK

Lincoln's two final sentences, and especially the very long last one (three times longer than the next longest sentence), explain what his addressees, "the living," ought to do instead of tarrying amidst the graves. They should "rather" (a word he repeats twice, echoing the adversative conjunction "but")—they should "rather" be "dedicated . . . to the unfinished work" and "the great task remaining."

These ultimate sentences of the Gettysburg Address have the very same structure as the last sentence of the second paragraph. Each begins with an anticipatory "it." Despite their parallel grammar, they convey opposite messages. It may be "altogether fitting and proper" to dedicate a cemetery, but Lincoln's conclusion is that we should instead dedicate ourselves to something larger. Substituting the deferred subject for the placeholder "it" yields an interesting, and rather unidiomatic, sentence: "To be dedicated here to the unfinished work . . . is **for us**." Remember that the effect of the deferred subject is to throw the weight of the sentence on whatever immediately follows the verb. Thus, the emphasis is placed on the prepositional phrase "for us." It is for us, the living, to do this. It belongs to us. It is ours. Lincoln is deepening and enlarging the meaning of what is proper. Dedicating the cemetery was a proper *thing* to do but dedicating *ourselves* is proper to us. The cause of self-government is proper to us as Americans, and proper to us as free and equal human beings. Lincoln moves from the observation of the proprieties—the rituals of burial—to the essential nature of the citizen and human being.

Richard Weaver, in his book *The Ethics of Rhetoric*, has noted that Lincoln favored what is called "the argument from definition." Even as a courtroom lawyer, Lincoln preferred to argue from first principles rather than from precedent. This tendency is nowhere more evident than in the First Inaugural, where, according to Weaver's analysis, Lincoln develops eight distinct arguments from definition (or genus) as he lays out the nature of government, the nature of contract, the nature of majority rule, the nature of popular sovereignty, and so on. As for the Gettysburg Address, Weaver indicates, in passing, that it departs from this dominant mode, instead being "based upon similitude." I think what Weaver means is that the burden of these three paragraphs is to remind the listener of the essential similarity of the living and the dead. The living slip readily into thinking of the dead—the heroic fathers, the martyred soldiers—as fundamentally unlike themselves, somehow better or nobler. Everett, for instance, spoke of the "wisest statesmen that ever lived" and "the purest patriots that ever died." Lincoln, however, insists on likeness. Our cause is the same as theirs; we must be what they were; we must act as they did. It is not enough for the nation to have been dedicated or for the cemetery to be dedicated; we must be dedicated.

DEDICATION AND RESOLVE

The dedication has multiple components, expressed in five clauses. Fascinatingly, these clauses, each beginning with "that," seem to parallel the famous clauses of the Declaration of Independence. Scott F. Crider, in *The Office of Assertion*, offers an analysis of the deep structure of the Declaration's parallel clauses, concluding that "It could be said that our country was invented with a fine sentence." If Jefferson's 110-word sentence invented the nation, Lincoln's 82-word parallel sentence reinvents it, turning truths into a task.

Declaration of Independence	Gettysburg Address
We hold these truths to be self-evident:	It is rather for us to be here dedicated to the great task remaining before us—
that all men are created equal;	**that** from these honored dead we take increased devotion to that cause for which they gave the last full measure of devotion—
that they are endowed by their Creator with certain inalienable rights;	**that** we here highly resolve
that among these are life, liberty, and the pursuit of happiness;	**that** these dead shall not have died in vain—
that to secure these rights, governments are instituted among men, deriving their just powers from the consent of the governed;	**that** this nation, under God, shall have a new birth of freedom—

> that whenever any form of government becomes destructive of these ends, it is the right of the people to alter or to abolish it and to institute new government, laying its foundation on such principles, and organizing its powers in such form, as to them shall seem most likely to effect their safety and happiness.

> and that government of the people, by the people, for the people, shall not perish from the earth.

As the sentence unfolds, Lincoln urges his listeners beyond "dedication" to "devotion" and finally to "resolve." Dedicate, devote, consecrate, and hallow: these verbs that bespeak solemn commitment to a higher purpose are all synonyms, and all more or less religious in tone. Resolve, however, whether used as a verb or a noun, is a different kind of word—a practical word that has both mathematical and political applications. "To resolve" can mean to find a solution for or to decide by vote. There are, of course, other prominent mathematical/scientific terms in the Gettysburg Address. After beginning with the founding **proposition** in the first paragraph, Lincoln compared the Civil War to a **test** of that proposition before sketching his solution in the final sentence. The answer to the question of whether the nation will endure is to be found through **resolve**. To be effective, dedication and devotion must take the form of resolve.

Resolve (or resolution) is a virtue that Lincoln had been interested in, I suspect, ever since he read Benjamin Franklin's *Autobiography* as a youngster. In his enumeration of the moral virtues, Franklin includes "Resolution," defining it as "Resolve to perform what you ought. Perform without fail what you resolve." The word figures significantly in Lincoln's Temperance Address, delivered on Washington's birthday in 1842, and more revealingly in a highly personal letter written to his friend Joshua Speed on July 4th of that same year. Responding to Speed's counsel on romantic matters about which Lincoln felt great perturbation, Lincoln writes:

> I acknowledge the correctness of your advice too; but before I resolve to do the one thing or the other, I must regain my confidence in my own ability to keep my resolves when they are made. In that ability, you know, I once prided myself as the only, or at least the chief, gem of my character; that gem I lost—how, and where, you too well know. I have not yet regained it; and until I do, I can not trust myself in any matter of much importance.

Lincoln admits no separation between private failings and public untrustworthiness. Character is of one piece; to Lincoln's mind, his broken engagement to Mary Todd (his eventual wife) spoke against his character altogether. His greatest biographer, Lord Charnwood, is more generous: "No shrewd judge of men could read his letters to Speed with care and not feel that, whatever mistakes this man might commit, fundamentally he was worthy of entire trust." Certainly, Lincoln's fixity of purpose (marital and political) was restored. Democratic statesmen, however, depend on more than their own resolve. They must awaken the resolve of citizens. The alternative, brilliantly described by Churchill in his "Locust Years" speech, is a government "resolved to be irresolute."

Thus, more significant than the mathematical valence of the

word "resolve" is its political import. In calling for resolve, Lincoln is evoking the language of legislation: "be it resolved that." This is a language he had been speaking since 1834, when at age twenty-five he was elected to the Illinois House of Representatives. One could, with relative ease, reformat the Gettysburg Address as a legislative resolution, with an opening series of "whereas" clauses, followed by a "be it resolved" clause. Lincoln's fidelity to republicanism is visible not only in his wonderful formulations—"new birth of freedom" and "government of the people, by the people, for the people"—but also, and maybe more fundamentally, in the trusting manner by which he addresses fellow citizens. Letting them know what needs to be done and how it can be done, he leaves it to them. Remarkably, he manages to summon and direct collective resolve while remaining nearly invisible himself, placed among and subsumed within the "we." In so many of his presidential speeches, but especially in the Gettysburg Address, Lincoln recedes from view. The first-person singular pronoun "I" is nowhere encountered. His speech displays the transcendence of self that he hopes to bring forth in others.

It may be unfair to compare contemporary politicians to Lincoln, but still there is no greater difference between him and them than the vanity, boastfulness, and almost clinical narcissism that they daily display. In the twentieth century, and especially its second half, the average employment of self-referential pronouns by American presidents has risen precipitously. Humility has disappeared as an element of rhetoric—forgotten perhaps because the virtue itself is increasingly rare. Humility is in no way at odds with loftiness of aim. After all, mere personal fame and fortune are not particularly lofty, whereas the achievement of self-government is.

In the Gettysburg Address, Lincoln calls upon the living to resolve three things: 1) "that these dead shall not have died in vain," 2) "that this nation, under God, shall have a new birth of freedom," and 3) "that government of the people, by the people, for the people, shall not perish from the earth." Although all three resolutions are, as they must be, in the future tense, the first and third are also formulated in the negative. We have two "shall nots" surrounding a "shall" (again suggestive of a balance between the conserving and progressing tendencies). The first "shall not" looks backward. We must push on to victory for the sake of the fallen. We do this in remembrance of them, so their sacrifice will not have been needless. Lincoln binds his listeners not just to the fathers in piety but devotedly to one another: the brave men "here," the honored dead "here." F. Scott Fitzgerald concluded his short story "The Swimmers" by saying that America, "having about it still that quality of the idea, was harder to utter—it was the graves at Shiloh and the tired, drawn, nervous faces of its great men. . . . It was a willingness of the heart." Of course, there are times when more patriot graves are not the solution. The reason more of that "last full measure of devotion" is called for "here" (repeated eight times like a drumbeat) is entwined with "that cause" for which "these honored dead" died.

Skipping for the moment over the second resolution, the final resolution explains "that cause" as the fate of self-government. We continue the fight so that "government of the people, by the people, for the people, shall not perish from the earth." Although Lincoln uses the future tense, his words do not soar into the empyrean. Not perishing is the aim. Lincoln is concerned as much with the survival as with the perfection of democracy. Yet, survival isn't a small aim; it might even be earth-shaking, since the Union preserved will constitute the needed proof that a nation conceived in liberty and dedicated to the proposition of equality can indeed endure. The Union has moral content and is worth saving.

What do Lincoln's weighty prepositions (government **of**, **by**, and **for** the people) tell us about that moral content? Another quick grammar reminder (from Sister Miriam Joseph's *The Trivium*): "a preposition unites substantives." It indicates the relations between things.[5] Lincoln is a master of prepositions, using ten different ones in the Gettysburg Address: above (once), before (once), by (once), for (five times), from (twice), in (four times), of (five times), on (twice), to (eight times), and under (once). In his most memorable parade of prepositions, Lincoln specifies three different ways that government and people can be joined or compounded together. Giving these relations a Lockean gloss, I would say that government **of** the people refers to the initial formation of the body politic—legitimate government is based on the consent **of** the governed; government **by** the people refers to the specific form that consent takes in a constitutional democracy, where there is ongoing consent through regular elections **by** the people; finally, government **for** the people means **for** their benefit—government must pursue the common good.

Mightily significant is a preposition Lincoln did not employ, namely "over." Government is not **over** the people. The Declaration of Independence as well had been careful to avoid any hint of dominance, stating that "governments are instituted

among men, deriving their just powers **from** the consent **of** the governed." It is only illegitimate government that manifests relations of over and under; thus, the Declaration espies "a Design to reduce them **under** absolute Despotism" and to establish "an absolute Tyranny **over** these States." Lincoln followed suit in reserving "over" for descriptions of abuse and unfairness. A few examples: At Peoria, he speaks of the "degrading" constitutional relations between the slave and free states as a result of the three-fifths clause, which gave "all the citizens of the slave States" an advantage "**over** those of the free." In the *Dred Scott* speech, referring to the fearful situation of slave women who are "left subject to the forced concubinage of their masters," Lincoln denounces "this particular power which they hold **over** their female slaves." Often, Lincoln speaks of the spread of slavery as a spreading of slavery **over** freedom, as in this passage from an 1859 speech in Columbus, Ohio, describing the disastrous consequences of the doctrine that "there is a perfect right according to interest to do just as you please":

> They will be ready for Jeff. Davis and Stephens and other leaders of that company, to sound the bugle for the revival of the slave trade, for the second Dred Scott decision, for the flood of slavery to be poured **over** the free States, while we shall be here tied down and helpless and run **over** like sheep.

Finally, after his 1864 re-election, Lincoln gave another extemporaneous response to a serenade, combining his dislike of "over" with the consensual resolve he had asked for in the Gettysburg Address: "It is no pleasure to me to triumph **over** any one; but I give thanks to the Almighty for this evidence of

the people's resolution to stand by free government and the rights of humanity."

FREEDOM ANEW

What, then, of the central resolution—the "shall" rather than the "shall not"—"that we here highly resolve . . . that this nation, under God, shall have a new birth of freedom"? Were we justified in delaying our discussion of it? Perhaps survival—the not-perishing of the third resolve—is dependent on the realization of this second resolve. Whereas the second relates to "this nation," the third relates to "government" (of the people-centered type). Is it only through "a new birth of freedom" experienced by "this nation" that self-government is sustainable? Much depends on the meaning of "a new birth of freedom."

It's natural and predictable for us today to hear in "a new birth of freedom" a foreshadowing of the perfected Constitution containing the 13th, 14th, and 15th Amendments. It is certainly true that, by November 1863, the Emancipation Proclamation had been in effect for almost a year, which meant that if the Union prevailed, slavery, at least, would be abolished. The further steps of Black citizenship and suffrage were more uncertain. Yet, it is also true that, as early as the Peoria Address, Lincoln had sketched the radical logic of the Declaration. In the center of that longest of his speeches, Lincoln had quoted the self-evident truths paragraph of the Declaration, adding his own emphatic highlighting by placing in all capitals the phrase "DERIVING THEIR JUST POWERS FROM THE CONSENT OF THE GOVERNED." After indicating that "the relation of masters and slaves is . . . a total violation of this principle," Lincoln drew the only logical conclusion: "Allow ALL the governed an equal voice in the government, and that, and that only, is self-government." Having made that bold statement, Lincoln had to backpedal immediately, announcing that he was not contending for political equality. As he put it in 1854: "I am not **now** combating the argument of NECESSITY"—that necessity being the fact of slavery and its legality under state law. By 1863, however, the necessity of slavery had been replaced by the necessity of emancipation. The dramatic shift in circumstances, through the course of the war, allowed Lincoln to press forward into public view, cautiously but persistently, the fullest implication of the consent principle. With Blacks now numbered entirely among free men, they were also entitled to an equal voice in government.

In a public letter of August 1863 (usually known as the Conkling letter), Lincoln was already preparing white public opinion to consider the civic claims of African Americans. In the final paragraph, the president explains what the triumph of the Union will mean:

> It will then have been proved that, among free men, there can be no successful appeal from the ballot to the bullet; and that they who take such appeal are sure to lose their case, and pay the cost. And then, there will be some black men who can remember that, with silent tongue, and clenched teeth, and steady eye, and well-poised bayonet, they have helped mankind on to this great consummation; while, I fear, there will be some white ones, unable to forget that, with malignant heart, and deceitful speech, they have strove to hinder it.

Despite the fact that Lincoln got the past perfect tense of "strive" wrong, many have recognized the beauty and power of this passage. Indeed, the letter quickly became tremendously popular, circulating in pamphlet form. What has not been sufficiently recognized is that this appreciation of the soldiers already contains the essentials of Lincoln's brief for Black suffrage. Lincoln explains that the principle for which the war was fought was the principle of free elections. In their contribution to Union victory, Black troops used the bullet to vindicate and re-establish the ballot. Reliance on the ballot is the principle that prevails "among free men."

Usually when scholars describe the evolution of Lincoln's policy positions—moving from support for colonization to support for arming Blacks to eventual support for Black suffrage (expressed in his final public words just days before the assassination)—they present this movement as if it entailed a significant shift of premises. They believe that Lincoln experienced a change of heart, contingent on a reconsideration of Black rights and capacities. Not so. While each policy position was calibrated to what white public opinion would sustain at a given moment, each was also clearly linked to and justified by the principles of the Declaration and proceeded upon the assumption that Blacks, like all people, were capable of self-government.

At the very end of the *Dred Scott* speech, Lincoln mentions colonization, stating explicitly that support for it depends on granting that "the negro is a man." Lincoln mentions the Exodus as a model of colonization. The metaphor casts white America explicitly in the role of the Egyptians, with Blacks as "the children of Israel." Here's what Lincoln says about that enslaved people: "The children of Israel, to such numbers as to include four hundred thousand fighting men, went out of Egyptian bondage in a body." Certainly, the metaphor serves Lincoln's aim by reminding his biblically steeped listeners of Egypt's punishment and of the possibility of a large-scale migration. But why mention the "four hundred thousand fighting men" among these "children of Israel"? The Bible verse that Lincoln must be referring to (Exodus 12:37) speaks only of the number "on foot that were men." By describing men on foot as if they were foot soldiers and then highlighting these infantrymen, Lincoln seems to be encouraging his white audience to be aware of how many fighting men there would be among the four million slaves held in American bondage. Lincoln's 1863 appreciation of the almost 200,000 Black soldiers who fought for their own freedom and for the principle of free government accords with his pre-war reflections on the "fighting men" among an enslaved people. Whether recommending independent Black nationhood or integration into the American polity, Lincoln acknowledged Black agency.

The movement of the Gettysburg Address is both linear—transitioning from past to present to future—and cyclical—revolving from birth to death to rebirth. And yet, it doesn't inscribe quite a full circle. We might wonder how the "new birth," which is a birth "of freedom," differs from the original birth, which was the birth of "a new nation." Is the liberty spoken of in the speech's opening the same as or different from the freedom spoken of at its end? The liberty of the opening was associated with conception, not birth, whereas freedom itself is now the thing born. Why this intriguing shift from "conceived in Liberty" to "a new birth of freedom"? And how does the new birth of freedom relate to equality?

In the earlier speculations about the meaning of "conceived in Liberty," three possibilities were floated: conceived in love of liberty, conceived in an act of liberty, or conceived in the setting of English liberty. None of those possibilities implied that all men would secure their natural right to liberty in the new nation. In other words, "conceived in Liberty" did not guarantee equality of liberty. Of the authors of the Declaration, Lincoln said (in his *Dred Scott* speech): "They did not mean to assert the obvious untruth, that all were then actually enjoying that equality, nor yet, that they were about to confer it immediately upon them. In fact they had no power to confer such a boon. They meant simply to declare the *right*, so that the *enforcement* of it might follow as fast as circumstances should permit." During the Civil War, circumstances had changed dramatically—such that the original conception in liberty could progress toward the actual birth of freedom as a consequence of the renewed dedication to equality. Freedom was a long time in gestation and it seemed like the nation might miscarry. Walt Whitman picked up on this birth imagery in his great oration, first delivered in 1879, on the "Death of Abraham Lincoln." There Whitman spoke of emancipation as "that parturition and delivery of our at last really free Republic, born again, henceforth to commence its career of genuine homogeneous Union, compact, consistent with itself."

It's important for us to remember that the freedom Lincoln heralds is an infant freedom, in need of further maturation. In part, this means freedom will grow and spread as it did with the adoption of the 15th, 19th, and 26th Amendments. But maturation also means the acquisition of moral and intellectual virtue through the disciplines of habit and study. As a nation, we have done better in extending freedom than in educating for it. In any case, as Lincoln foresees, there will always be plenty for future generations to do. This may be one of the reasons the Gettysburg Address is so beloved. It rallies us today just as it rallied the nation then.

In closing, we shouldn't overlook the presence of the phrase "under God." Whereas Lincoln rejected the application of "over" to the relation of government to people, he embraces it in the relation of nation to God (if the nation is under God, then God is over or above the nation). According to Lincoln, the superintendence of God plays a role in the new birth of freedom. The divinity, of course, is present in the opening proposition that "all men are *created* equal." According to the Declaration, our equality is connected with our creatureliness. The God of the Declaration (or at least the God of its opening paragraph) is explicitly "Nature's God," not necessarily the God of Abraham or the Triune God. One can believe in species-based human equality without believing in divine Providence or God's ongoing benevolent care for his creation. Lincoln's civic religion, however, brings God closer. "That nation" might not have been "under God," but "this nation"—rededicated and reborn—shall be. During his presidency, Lincoln issued three proclamations calling on citizens to observe a Day of National Humiliation, Prayer, and Fasting, in addition to his four Thanksgiving Proclamations (two establishing the holiday tradition and two others giving thanks to "the Divine Majesty" for victories). Lincoln's hint here of a politically active, justice-seeking, providential order, setting certain limits upon human action, will come to fruition in his Second Inaugural. That speech, Lincoln knew, was his greatest, outvying even the Gettysburg Address.

The Second Inaugural

1619 and Charity for All

If Gettysburg is Lincoln's war speech, then the Second Inaugural is his peace speech. Yet, each confounds expectations. We have seen how Lincoln pursued victory without the usual resort to vilification. To vindicate the cause of self-government, the national bonds of affection would have to be revived; accordingly, Lincoln had said nothing at Gettysburg to imperil a return to friendship. In the Second Inaugural, with the end of the war almost in view, Lincoln turns to the achievement of "a just, and a lasting peace, among ourselves." He does not endorse the path of forgetting, simply setting aside differences and burying the hatchet. But neither does he recommend a punitive apportioning of blame. Just as he fought the war with resolution rather than fervor, he wages the peace with charity rather than pride.

Yet before charity could be possible, it was necessary to understand what had happened. Reconciliation requires truth-telling and an inquiry into the cause and purpose of the war.

Thus, in his Second Inaugural, Lincoln insists on revisiting the conflict—both its outbreak in 1861 and its ultimate origin in 1619. He offers an interpretation of the Civil War that, if accepted by all, would unite whites, North and South, in humility before God's judgment upon "American Slavery" and that would, in consequence, create the civic space in which Blacks could unite with whites. The former bondsmen could be encompassed within newly forged bonds of affection.

The Second Inaugural is the original and better 1619 Project. Both share the conviction that Americans must fully feel and acknowledge the nation's foundational wrong, not only by confessing but by doing—doing, in fact, **all** that is requisite for peace and justice. The speech differs, however, from the recent revisionism in decisive ways. Lincoln's approach manifests not only greater historical accuracy but also greater psychological realism and political prudence. He is acutely aware of the dispositional obstacles that impede reconciliation: the temptations of northern moralistic arrogance, southern regressive resentment, white race hatred, and Black rage. His interpretation of the war is designed to blunt the force of each of these passions. His is the spirit of reparative atonement without animus or malice.

Fellow Countrymen:

At this second appearing to take the oath of the presidential office, there is less occasion for an extended address than there was at the first. Then a statement, somewhat in detail, of a course to be pursued, seemed fitting and proper. Now, at the expiration of four years, during which

public declarations have been constantly called forth
on every point and phase of the great contest which still
absorbs the attention, and engrosses the energies of the
nation, little that is new could be presented. The progress
of our arms, upon which all else chiefly depends, is as well
known to the public as to myself; and it is, I trust, reasonably satisfactory and encouraging to all. With high hope
for the future, no prediction in regard to it is ventured.

On the occasion corresponding to this four years ago,
all thoughts were anxiously directed to an impending
civil-war. All dreaded it—all sought to avert it. While the
inaugeral address was being delivered from this place,
devoted altogether to *saving* the Union without war,
insurgent agents were in the city seeking to *destroy* it
without war—seeking to dissolve the Union, and divide
effects, by negotiation. Both parties deprecated war; but
one of them would *make* war rather than let the nation
survive; and the other would *accept* war rather than let it
perish. And the war came.

One eighth of the whole population were colored
slaves, not distributed generally over the Union, but
localized in the Southern part of it. These slaves constituted a peculiar and powerful interest. All knew that
this interest was, somehow, the cause of the war. To
strengthen, perpetuate, and extend this interest was the
object for which the insurgents would rend the Union,
even by war; while the government claimed no right to

do more than to restrict the territorial enlargement of it. Neither party expected for the war, the magnitude, or the duration, which it has already attained. Neither anticipated that the *cause* of the conflict might cease with, or even before, the conflict itself should cease. Each looked for an easier triumph, and a result less fundamental and astounding. Both read the same Bible, and pray to the same God; and each invokes His aid against the other. It may seem strange that any men should dare to ask a just God's assistance in wringing their bread from the sweat of other men's faces; but let us judge not that we be not judged. The prayers of both could not be answered; that of neither has been answered fully. The Almighty has His own purposes. "Woe unto the world because of offences! for it must needs be that offences come; but woe to that man by whom the offence cometh!" If we shall suppose that American Slavery is one of those offences which, in the providence of God, must needs come, but which, having continued through His appointed time, He now wills to remove, and that He gives to both North and South, this terrible war, as the woe due to those by whom the offence came, shall we discern therein any departure from those divine attributes which the believers in a Living God always ascribe to Him? Fondly do we hope—fervently do we pray—that this mighty scourge of war may speedily pass away. Yet, if God wills that it continue, until all the wealth piled by the bond-man's two hundred and fifty years of unrequited toil shall be sunk, and until every drop of blood drawn with the lash, shall be paid by another drawn with the sword, as was said three thousand years ago, so still it must be said "the judgments of the Lord, are true and righteous altogether."

With malice toward none; with charity for all; with firmness in the right, as God gives us to see the right, let us strive on to finish the work we are in; to bind up the nation's wounds; to care for him who shall have borne the battle, and for his widow, and his orphan—to do all which may achieve and cherish a just, and a lasting peace, among ourselves, and with all nations.

THE ART OF THE SINKING SELF

Among inaugural addresses, Lincoln's Second is anomalous. When delivered on March 4, 1865, more than three decades had passed since the last such occasion. Nonetheless, since five of the first seven presidents served a second term, a sort of formula had emerged for the shape of a repeat inaugural. The opening centered on the speaker, with an acknowledgement of the oath-taking and the public's renewed trust. Re-elected presidents made free use of "me, myself, and I," usually to express their gratitude, heightened sense of responsibility, and attention to future efforts. George Washington, for instance, included nine first-person singular pronouns in his impossibly brief, 133-word speech. In the special case of inaugural addresses, this density of self-reference is not indicative of egoism but is instead linked to the occasion's purpose: the binding by oath of a person to a constitutional office. Thus, Washington says,

> This oath I am now about to take, and in your presence: That if it shall be found during my administration of the Government I have in any instance violated willingly or knowingly the injunctions thereof, I may (besides incurring constitutional punishment) be subject to the upbraidings of all who are now witnesses of the present solemn ceremony.

Stern stuff.

Lincoln's First Inaugural, delivered on March 4, 1861, had been similarly framed around the oath of office. His opening sentence noted the constitutional requirement of the oath, as well as the custom of administering the oath publicly. At the end of the speech, Lincoln circled back to the oath, bringing its meaning to bear on the difference between his duty-bound situation and the choice facing his "dissatisfied fellow countrymen." Firmly, he told them, "*You* have no oath registered in Heaven to destroy the government, while *I* shall have the most solemn one to 'preserve, protect and defend' it." Lincoln meant for this to be the final sentence. The late addition of a more poetic ending— attempting to sound those "mystic chords of memory" by appeal to "the better angels of our nature"—was William Seward's idea. While the editorial intervention by the incoming secretary of state gave the world a beautiful piece of prose (once Seward's flatfooted version was reworked by Lincoln), the additional paragraph impaired the tight structure of the original. "Prescribed by the Constitution," the presidential oath is strengthened by a democratic "custom as old as the government itself," and ultimately "registered in Heaven." By bookending the First Inaugural with these references, Lincoln let it be known that his range of political maneuver was limited by the superior authorities of Constitution, custom, and God.

The Second Inaugural does not neglect the oath; Lincoln begins by mentioning it. After that, however, he ticks none of the usual inaugural boxes (gratitude for the honor, review of policy successes, sketch of promise ahead). Of course, there was nothing normal about a national election in time of civil war, with voters in only twenty-five of the thirty-six states participating. Expecting a loss and fearing the worst for the Union in that eventuality, Lincoln nonetheless insisted on the canvass (not, by the way, the choice an aspiring tyrant would make). Two days after his re-election, greeting yet another band of serenaders, Lincoln made the sort of statement one might have expected him to revisit and refine for his Second Inaugural, just as his Gettysburg Address had wrought to perfection the themes of his extemporaneous post-battle remarks. In this November 10 speech, Lincoln explains why a republic already undergoing a "severe test" had to accept the additional strain of an election, inevitably pitting a war party against a peace-at-any-cost party:

> If the loyal people, *united*, were put to the utmost of their strength by the rebellion, must they not fail when *divided*, and partially paralyzed, by a political war among themselves?
>
> But the election was a necessity.
>
> We can not have free government without elections; and if the rebellion could force us to forego, or postpone a national

election, it might fairly claim to have already conquered and ruined us.

Continuing with talk of the "good" the election has done in demonstrating "how *sound*, and how *strong* we still are," he closes with a call to "re-unite in a common effort, to save our common country." Striving to repair the electoral strife, Lincoln pleads with his own side to join him in magnanimity: "So long as I have been here I have not willingly planted a thorn in any man's bosom. . . . May I ask those who have not differed with me, to join with me, in this same spirit towards those who have?"

Four months later, at the time of the inauguration, with the military situation much improved, the task of reunification had enlarged well beyond the parties to the election; it now included all parties to the war. The ultimate message of not planting thorns (and removing those already embedded) remains the same, but the rhetorical difficulty has increased many-fold. In response, Lincoln no longer features himself or any of his homely unaffected metaphors. Given the occasion, his studied avoidance of self-reference is difficult to execute. Indeed, the attempt to sink himself from view leads him into a rare grammatical error. In the last sentence of the opening paragraph, speaking of the "progress of our arms," Lincoln says, "With high hope for the future, no prediction in regard to it is ventured." The modifier dangles. As written, the "no prediction" is the entity that has high hope. The logical impossibility could be fixed in various ways, but the most direct would be to switch to the active voice (that standard recommendation for better writing), as in, "with high hope for the future, I yet venture no prediction."

Even before his self-suppression reached the point of ungrammatical unclarity, Lincoln was giving the passive voice quite a workout. George Washington began his Second Inaugural with admirable straightforwardness: "I am again called upon by the voice of my country to execute the functions of its Chief Magistrate." Lincoln, by contrast, says: "At this second appearing to take the oath of the presidential office, there is less occasion for an extended address than there was at the first." While avoiding "I" like the plague, Lincoln cannot entirely avoid self-reference. It is, after all, his second appearing. While not as miraculous as the Second Coming, "this second appearing" has a disembodied or ghostly quality because of his refusal to center himself as the subject of the sentence.[1] Think of the alternative: "As I come before you a second time to take the oath, I find less need for an extended address." The oddity of Lincoln's first sentence should alert us that he is attempting something unique and untried.

Echoing the depreciation of speech in relation to deed of the Gettysburg Address, Lincoln warns us that this speech, too, will be brief. The focus of the first sentence is on the address itself—or rather, it is on the difference in length between the addresses associated with his first and second appearings. Lincoln immediately jumps back to that moment, "then," in 1861, when fuller speech was (or at least "seemed") "fitting and proper." Here Lincoln borrows a phrase he used once (and only once) before to describe a speech act. This repetition of the Gettysburg phrase links the more extended address of his First Inaugural, which "seemed fitting and proper" at that time, to the official dedication at Gettysburg, which was "altogether fitting and proper." By reminding the audience of these two earlier speeches, he enchains these three major presidential addresses together.

Although Lincoln began his First Inaugural by saying, "I appear before you to address you briefly," he then spoke at some length and was, in fact, unwilling to quit the podium, confiding to his audience and to posterity, "I am loth to close." Why loth? Aware that once he stopped talking, "the momentous issue of civil war" would be in the hands of his "dissatisfied fellow countrymen," Lincoln was not at all confident that his plea to "think calmly and well" would be heeded. One imagines "I am loth to close" was spoken with aching poignancy. Persuasion must be attempted even though secession had already precluded success. Speech "then" was "fitting and proper," but "now," in 1865, speech is a matter of "less" and "little"—"there is less occasion" for it and "little that is new could be presented." The echoes of Gettysburg continue to reverberate: this second echo (disparaging the value of speech) links the "little" of the Second Inaugural with the "little" of Gettysburg ("the world will little note . . . what we say here"). Just as at the cemetery, Lincoln pivots from words to deeds—to "the progress of our arms, upon which all else chiefly depends." Lincoln will again leverage these deeds of bravery for the future. The high resolve called for at the close of the Gettysburg Address becomes the "let us strive on" in the final sentence of the Second Inaugural. It will, however, take some impressive talk, of a very different order, to bring his audience to this new consummation.

Another reason a standard inaugural update is unnecessary is that there has been no shortage of speech during Lincoln's tenure in office. Stressing how well-informed the public is, as well-informed as himself, Lincoln finally does use the words "myself" and "I," but only in order to make the point that president and public are equally knowledgeable. This is not an apathetic public: "the great contest . . . still absorbs the attention, and engrosses the energies of the nation." Nor is it a secretive administration: "public declarations have been constantly called forth on every point and phase." Interestingly, Lincoln presents these public declarations not as issued by his administration but instead as "called forth"—one presumes by public demand. There is perhaps another, very faint, echo of Gettysburg in this mention of public declarations "called forth" by a self-governing people. This is the daily living out of the Declaration "brought forth" by the fathers.

Lincoln's assertion that the public knows as much as the commander in chief about "the progress of our arms" gives evidence of what might today be called "government transparency." The claim of transparency, however, involves a measure of concealment as well. Lincoln does not say that the public knows as much as he does about the planning and execution of military strategy. The public sees only the visible result, the forward march of Union forces. About that "progress," Lincoln says, "it is, I trust, reasonably satisfactory and encouraging." By subordinating himself in this little parenthetical, Lincoln understates not only the incipient victory but his commanding role in that victory. This absence of gloating or glorying has been noted by many commentators; perhaps nothing proves it so much as this relegation of himself to an aside.[2]

DEMOCRACY AND THE ALL

What replaces "I" as the operative actor? In the Gettysburg Address, where Lincoln also caused himself to disappear, he relied heavily on "we." By contrast, in the Second Inaugural, although "we" appears, it is not used with nearly the same frequency. "We" appears ten times in the Gettysburg Address (the most used word other than "that" and "the"). Accounting for the different lengths of the speeches, "we" would need to appear twenty-three times to equal the Gettysburg rate. Instead, it appears six times, clustered in the speech's second half. What replaces either "I" or "we"—both definite pronouns—is the indefinite pronoun "all." "All" is far and away the most frequently used word in the Second Inaugural, appearing ten times. In addition, there are words that resonate with "all," such as "altogether" (twice), "always" (once), and "Almighty" (once).

"I" often implies "not-I," just as "we" often implies "not-we," which is to say "they." Although Lincoln did not mention the rebels in the Gettysburg Address, it was—as a war speech— structured by this us/them dichotomy. There was an implicit distinction between the loyal and disloyal dead, just as there was an explicit distinction between "we" ("the living") and "they"— repeated three times in reference to the "honored dead," whose devotion to "that cause" we must imitate. There is no "they" in the Second Inaugural. Instead, there is an "all." "All" denotes some whole quantity, whether of persons or things. The Second Inaugural is a speech about the whole, about how to put "the whole population" of a fractured country together. Of course, the Gettysburg Address also acknowledged the "all" of the nation's founding assertion. But because Lincoln spoke there to those whose loyalty to the Union rendered them receptive to a shared identity built upon a universal truth about universal human equality, he did not have to work quite as hard to find and assert commonality. In the Second Inaugural, Lincoln sets about discovering or constructing an "all" from discordant parts—not only the parties to the war but also the newly freed "one eighth of the whole." Lincoln must perforce acknowledge the existence of these heterogeneous parts, and the part each played in the war, yet do so without deepening the divisions. Hence, none is labeled a "they." In this endeavor—an endeavor both explanatory and ameliorative—he relies on other indefinite pronouns ("both," "each," "neither," the "one" and the "other"), but always he will place these within the unifying and homogenizing context of "all." Moreover, the whole to which "all" has reference will shift and expand as the argument of the address develops.

Long before the Second Inaugural, Lincoln had been using the word "all," often and well, with tremendous defining power. "All" is prominent in many (if not all) of his most famous formulations. Here's a sampler, tending to confirm his assertion that all his political feelings sprang from the "all" of the Declaration.

Allow **ALL** the governed an equal voice in the government, and that, and that only, is self-government. (Peoria Address, 1854)

They [the authors of the Declaration] meant to set up a standard maxim for free society, which could be familiar to **all**, and revered by **all**; constantly looked to, constantly labored for, and even though never perfectly attained, constantly approximated, and thereby constantly spreading and deepening its influence, and augmenting the happiness and value of life to **all** people of **all** colors everywhere. (*Dred Scott* speech, 1857)

All honor to Jefferson—to the man who, in the concrete pressure of a struggle for national independence by a single people, had the coolness, forecast, and capacity to introduce into a merely revolutionary document, an abstract truth, applicable to **all** men and **all** times, and so to embalm it there, that to-day, and in **all** coming days, it shall be a rebuke and a stumbling-block to the very harbingers of re-appearing tyranny and oppression. (Letter to Pierce, 1859)

That something, is the principle of "Liberty to **all**"—the principle that clears the *path* for **all**—gives *hope* to **all**—and, by consequence, *enterprize*, and *industry* to **all**. (Fragment on the Constitution and the Union, 1860)

This is essentially a people's contest. On the side of the Union, it is a struggle for maintaining in the world that form and substance of government whose leading object is to elevate the condition of men; to lift artificial weights from **all** shoulders; to clear the paths of laudable pursuit for **all**; to afford **all** an unfettered start and a fair chance in the race of life. (Message to Congress, 1861)

In the Second Inaugural, Lincoln's earlier experimentation with this most democratic word takes on a new level of rhetorical complexity, sustained throughout the speech.

BOTH PARTIES AND THE WAR

In the first paragraph, the group of people contained in the "all" are the Unionists. How do we know that? Well, in March 1865, the rebels certainly could not regard the military situation as "reasonably satisfactory and encouraging." They are not part of the "all" who are cheered by "the progress of our arms." Although noting the improved state of northern morale, Lincoln says nothing to heighten it. At Gettysburg, he labored to boost the fighting spirit; now, if anything, he tempers it, even tamps it down. While victory is necessary, it is subordinated to something Lincoln calls "all else." Avoiding specificity, Lincoln says that "all else chiefly depends" on this incipient military success. What is "all else"? Aristotle taught long ago that war should never be undertaken for its own sake. War is for the sake of peace. Is peace the "all else"? It is true that Lincoln will end the Second Inaugural with a vision of wide-spreading peace—peace that is both "just" and "lasting." The qualifiers, however, indicate that there are different kinds of peace; not every peace is worth pursuing. After all, the reason that Lincoln was taking the oath of office again was because the electorate had rejected the unjust brand of peace favored by that faction of the Democratic Party called the Copperheads or Peace Democrats.

Having foiled a peace settlement based on accepting either national dismemberment or Black re-enslavement, Lincoln might have been expected to use his inaugural to describe how he planned to proceed with "the re-inauguration of the national authority."[3] Instead, he indicates that he will not be elaborating on the "course to be pursued" in his second term. What, then, are the next three paragraphs intended to do? Although they do not constitute a policy statement or a legislative agenda for reconstruction, they are essentially political, in that they are concerned with securing the civic preconditions for "all else." Through his interpretation of the war, Lincoln strives to create a public sentiment—a conjoining of judgment and feeling—that will support the practical and immensely difficult work ahead. "All else" might "chiefly" depend on Grant and Sherman and the boys in blue, but whether a Confederate surrender leads to "a just, and a lasting, peace" will depend on the statesmanship of Lincoln and what can be accomplished through wise words.

As we've seen, the first paragraph toggles back and forth between "this second appearing" and "the first," back and forth between "Then" and "Now." Alternating between 1865 and 1861, the Second Inaugural begins from a much-compressed time horizon. This is quite unlike the sweeping linear arc of the Gettysburg Address, where the paragraphs move rapidly and sequentially through past (1776) to present to future. The Second Inaugural reverses the direction of inquiry. Starting from the present, it goes back into the past, eventually very far back. Like an archeologist, Lincoln begins by examining the surface layers of the war before uncovering the deeper deposits, like its underlying cause and hidden but central purpose. The second paragraph, which provides the surface account, is entirely set in the near past: specifically, March 4, 1861, "on the occasion corresponding to this four years ago."

Although whisking us back to his first inauguration, Lincoln continues to abstract from himself. He speaks of what was happening "while the inaugural address was being delivered from this place." Yet one wouldn't know from the construction of the sentence that he was the one delivering the address. The focus is on the thoughts, feelings, and actions of "all": "all thoughts were anxiously directed to an impending civil-war. All dreaded it—all sought to avert it." The word "all" now encompasses more than those loyal to the Union. It includes even the "insurgent agents." Finding this point of commonality, Lincoln insists that no one wanted war. The Civil War was not a result of warmongering. There were no bloodthirsty aggressors, no one spoiling for a fight.

There were, however, two parties. The first identification of the parties is curious, since Lincoln does not refer to a sectional division. Instead, the division is oddly localized within the District of Columbia: "While the inaugural address was being delivered from **this place**, devoted altogether to *saving* the Union without war, insurgent agents were **in the city** seeking to *destroy* it without war—seeking to dissolve the Union, and divide effects, by negotiation." What is "this place" to which Lincoln refers? And how can a place be devoted to saving the Union? Does he mean the Capitol building, personified to imply that the inaugural event had assembled together in one place the new Lincoln administration and the new Republican-controlled Congress? If so, it was the federal government as a whole that was "devoted altogether to *saving* the Union without war." Or, does he really mean the precise spot, the East Portico of the Capitol, from which the inaugural address was delivered? In that case, it would be Lincoln himself, who occupied that place, who was "devoted altogether to *saving* the Union without war." Pressing himself out of view has once again created a kind of obscurity in his account of events.

The description of the other side is curious also. Lincoln does not refer generally to the secessionists or to the ordinances of secession issued by state conventions and governments. By the time of the inauguration, seven states had taken such unconstitutional and provocative action, with South Carolina leading the van on December 20, 1860, and Texas bringing up the rear on February 1, 1861. Instead of focusing on the states, Lincoln describes "insurgent agents" who were "in the city." They were there, in Washington, "seeking to dissolve the Union"—not by secession apparently but rather by "negotiation." By limiting the presentation so severely as to time and place, restricting it to March 4, 1861, in Washington, D.C., Lincoln seems to be leaving a lot out of his account of the origins of the war. During the months that leaders throughout the Deep South were committing their states to secession, there were numerous attempts to avert the "impending civil-war" through some sort of negotiated settlement that would guarantee slavery in perpetuity. However, by the time Lincoln took office, these initiatives, like the Crittenden Compromise and the February Peace Conference at the Willard Hotel, had failed. Moreover, Lincoln's resolute opposition to these legislative schemes (on the grounds that they would have effectively invalidated the will of the people as expressed through the recent election) had helped put the kibosh on them. Just as peace at any price is not desirable, neither is compromise at any cost. After the Confederate States of America had incorporated itself in early February, it did indeed send agents to Washington with the aim of negotiating a treaty to "divide effects," as Lincoln says. From the Confederate perspective, the premise of such negotiations was an already existing separation. From Lincoln's perspective, "in view of the Constitution and the laws," as he explained in the First Inaugural, "the Union is unbroken." There was no Confederacy, only a "so-called confederacy."

Having begun the second paragraph by noting that "all" were anxious about the war, Lincoln at the same time limited the actors to a handful of insurgent agents and himself (or perhaps the U.S. government). The next sentence, however, generalizes or widens the conflict to "both parties." Lincoln must now be referring to the larger grouping that stands behind the insurgent agents who are on site in the federal district. This party "would *make* war rather than let the nation survive," whereas "the other would *accept* war rather than let it perish." This dynamic between the party of extinction and the party of preservation produced a result: "And the war came." What was impending happened.

Despite the unclarity in the middle sentence, a few points emerge from this second paragraph. First, no one wanted war. Second, the conflict was over the Union, whether it should be destroyed or saved. Third, although no one wanted war, the war was nonetheless the consequence of human actions and choices. One party was prepared to make war and the other prepared to accept war. Each had something in view that it regarded as more important than avoiding war, something important enough to justify war. Fourth, war was a consequence, a logical result, not happenstance or a mistake.

Many scholars are struck by the moral evenhandedness of Lincoln's presentation. I see that quality but would urge against overestimating it. Lincoln's reliance on indefinite pronouns ("all," "both," "one," and "the other") generates an impression of impartiality and equivalence. However, there is an undeniable moral judgment expressed toward the parties. The insurgent agents, as well as the party who sent them, have set their faces against the nation's survival; they are actively seeking "to *destroy* it." The other side refuses to allow the nation to "perish" and is "devoted altogether to *saving* the Union." Reverberating again are echoes of Gettysburg in the words "devoted" and "perish," as well as echoes of the republic-destroyers and republic-savers prefigured in the Lyceum Address.

Despite these sharp discriminations, the judgment conveyed by the presentation is softened or elided in certain respects. By

not rehashing (as I have done) the pre-inaugural course of secession and not mentioning who fired the first shots at Fort Sumter,
Lincoln lessens or diffuses blame for the war. He doesn't excuse
the insurgents—the term connotes censure—but insurgents are
distinct from belligerents. Lincoln does not place sole or dispro-
portionate blame for the war on the insurgents. It took "both
parties," acting as they did for the reasons they did, to produce
the war that both deprecated.

THE CAUSE OF THE CONFLICT

Paragraph two explains the outbreak of the war, but it does not
address its cause. The deeper matter of causation is the topic to
which Lincoln turns in the long and stunning third paragraph.

A note here about the structure of the Second Inaugural: It is
composed of twenty-six sentences distributed among four paragraphs. The first two paragraphs are each composed of five sentences. The much longer third paragraph has fifteen sentences.
The fourth paragraph is just one complex sentence. Analysis of
the dense third paragraph requires discerning its subsections.
Arguably, Lincoln could have split this paragraph in two. The
most obvious dividing line, recognized by many commentators,
is the paragraph's shortest sentence: "The Almighty has His
own purposes." This sentence serves as a kind of fulcrum, the
point at which the causal analysis shifts from a purely human
perspective to a viewpoint *sub specie aeternitatis*. Taking this as
the pivot, the third paragraph is composed of a section of ten
sentences and a section of five sentences, with the two sections
having an almost identical word count (199/195). However, it
might have been just as defensible to split the paragraph three

sentences earlier, between the seventh and eighth sentences, for that is the moment at which religion is first introduced: "Both read the same Bible, and pray to the same God; and each invokes His aid against the other." Religion appears on the political scene because of the human behavior that seeks to muster God militarily. Another indication of the significance of this moment is that the verb tense within the paragraph shifts from past to present (a fact that does not become perfectly clear until the verb "pray," since the past and present tenses of "read" look identical on the page). Although there are definite subsections within the third paragraph, which must be unpacked in sequence, Lincoln rightly bundles them as part of one inquiry into the cause of the war.

The third paragraph begins with a part of the whole not yet mentioned: "One eighth of the whole population were colored slaves, not distributed generally over the Union, but localized in the Southern part of it." Lincoln highlights various features of this portion of the population: the number, the color, the condition, and the location of these residents are all important, but perhaps most important is simply the description of these persons as belonging to the whole. Lincoln speaks of slaves, not slavery. He focuses on real, countable human beings rather than an institution. Not being free citizens, these "colored slaves" have no say in their location; they are "distributed" rather than having chosen to live or reside somewhere. Note how careful Lincoln's phrasing is. He does not speak of the South but rather "the Southern part" of the Union. Over the course of the war, it might have been easy to slip into regarding the North as synonymous with the Union; Lincoln rejects that identification. The Union is the whole and the denizens of this "Southern part"— whether colored slaves or white citizens—are part of the whole.

Lincoln's description also indicates that slavery and color are entwined with one another. Not all colored people are enslaved, but all slaves are colored (or regarded as colored). Significantly, however, Lincoln does not use the word "race." Examination of his speeches from the 1850s shows that he generally avoided the term. By contrast, defenders of slavery routinely identified slaves as belonging to "the African race." Race language suggests the existence of essentially different categories (and in the mouths of white supremacists the implication of a race-based hierarchy). Lincoln's preferred language of "color" marks a visible difference, but one that is only skin deep and is, moreover, arrayed across a spectrum. Nonetheless, the fact that condition and color are linked makes this demographic stand out as a distinct and identifiable minority within the whole.

Slaves comprise an anomalous part. The next sentence provides further definition: "These slaves constituted a peculiar and powerful interest." The word "peculiar" had long been peculiarly associated with slavery. In a coinage traceable to John C. Calhoun, slavery was called the South's "peculiar institution"—a euphemism that was meant to convey southern specialness but that was also adopted, with heavy sarcasm, by slavery's opponents. (Frederick Douglass, for instance, was often introduced as a "graduate from the peculiar institution, with his diploma written on his back.") Lincoln has so far avoided using the word "slavery" or the word "institution." Instead, he speaks of "these slaves" as "a peculiar interest." This formulation captures the essence of enslavement: human beings become a commodity in which other human beings hold an economic interest. Without naming the commodifiers—the oligarchic few who were slave-owners and slave-dealers—he is penetrating to the motive behind the peculiar institution. Lincoln had done the same in speeches throughout the 1850s. Winding up the *Dred Scott* speech, he described how the meaning of the Declaration was obscured by the lust for profit: "the plainest print cannot be read through a gold eagle." An even more powerful denunciation was developed in an undated fragment of writing entitled "Pro-Slavery Theology"; its conclusion satirizes "the positive good" theory of slavery (another Calhoun contribution):

> But, slavery is good for some people!!! As a *good* thing, slavery is strikingly perculiar [*sic*],[4] in this, that it is the only good thing which no man ever seeks the good of, *for himself*.
>
> Nonsense! Wolves devouring lambs, not because it is good for their own greedy maws, but because it is good for the lambs!!!

After more accurately characterizing slave-ownership as an interest rather than an institution—and thereby reminding us of Madison's observation in Federalist 10 that interests are powerful drivers of political faction—Lincoln declares, "All knew that this interest was, somehow, the cause of the war." Once again, the knowledge of the public is stressed. The statement is unequivocal: "all knew," which is to say both those who shared the interest and those who did not were aware that "this interest" was the cause of the war. Although the cause was known to all, the operation of the cause is unspecific: this interest was "somehow" the cause of the war.

The next sentence provides considerably more detail about the "somehow," for it moves from the "all" (the point of agreement) to a specification of the divergent aims of the parties,

and especially the scope of those aims: "To strengthen, perpetuate, and extend this interest was the object for which the
insurgents would rend the Union, even by war; while the government claimed no right to do more than to restrict the territorial enlargement of it." Lincoln now clearly denominates the
parties as "the insurgents" and "the government." What was at
issue between them was whether "this interest"—the economic
system based on property in man—would spread, thereby becoming perpetual, or whether it would be confined to its existing localization.

Interestingly, Lincoln makes no reference to the party that
sought to end slavery immediately and comprehensively: the
abolitionists. Although he indicated on many occasions that he
found abolitionist extremism unhelpful, the abolitionists do not
figure here as either a cause of the conflict or one of the parties
to the war. Since Lincoln's focus is still on that moment in 1861
when the war came, this exclusion is perhaps accurate. By that
point, abolitionists were ranged on the side of the government,
despite their ferocious criticism of Lincoln's moderation. Lincoln's characterization of the government's position summarizes
the Republican Party's antebellum acceptance of the "federal
consensus," namely that there was no federal right to interfere
with slavery in the existing slave states, at the same time that (as
he said at Cooper Union) neither federalism nor the Constitution "forbid our *Federal Government* to control as to slavery in *our
Federal Territories*." In other words, the war arose from a policy
dispute over the extension or non-extension of "this interest."

Of course, the struggle over the political power and ultimate fate of "this interest" had been ongoing, with varying

degrees of intensity, since the constitutional convention in 1787. Thus, many of the major markers and episodes of U.S. history revolve around this struggle: the Northwest Ordinance, the Missouri Compromise, the nullification controversy, the Mexican-American War, the Compromise of 1850, the Kansas-Nebraska Act, and the *Dred Scott* decision. As the crisis escalated throughout the 1850s, Lincoln argued for a return to "the old policy of the fathers." Non-extension had been their anti-slavery strategy; Lincoln sought to reclaim that original ground as being both principled and prudent. Although he insisted on the conservatism of the Republicans, it was also true that for the first time in the nation's history an administration was in office whose entire reason for being was to prevent the spread of slavery by exercising the right to put "this interest" in lockdown and quarantine. Since the Peoria Address, Lincoln had used a disease metaphor comparing the slave interest to "a wen or a cancer" afflicting the body politic; this cancer, though not able to be immediately excised, might be treatable by isolating and containing it.

As in the second paragraph when "both parties" were first introduced, the next section of the Second Inaugural summarizes key similarities between them, similarities that persisted through the war:

> Neither party expected for the war, the magnitude, or the duration, which it has already attained. Neither anticipated that the cause of the conflict might cease with, or even before, the conflict itself should cease. Each looked for an easier triumph, and a result less fundamental and astounding.

In their overly confident initial expectations, they were equally mistaken. Interestingly, Lincoln uses scientific terms, measurements of space and time, to characterize the war. His diction ("magnitude" and "duration") encourages emotional distance from the terrible toll of the carnage, stressing instead how unexpected the force of the war was. The deficiencies of forethought extended to the fate in store for "the cause of the conflict." Would the insurgents really have made war if they had foreseen that their action would extinguish "their peculiar and powerful interest"? The government, too, did not anticipate (and thus could not be said to be seeking) this "fundamental and astounding" result. Although Lincoln became convinced that abolition was necessary to save the Union, he never conceived of the war as an abolition war. In fact, he believed it would have been a violation of his oath to have given the cause of abolition priority over the cause of Union (as the abolitionists did). Although referring to the abolition of slavery effected largely by the Emancipation Proclamation of 1863 and fully by the 13th Amendment of 1865, Lincoln speaks in a kind of code, still not using the words "slavery" or "abolition."

It is perhaps somewhat surprising to hear Lincoln say that "Each looked for . . . a result less fundamental and astounding," given that the result the insurgents looked for was the break-up of the United States. In the face of all he said at Gettysburg, Lincoln now declares that the abolition of slavery is more fundamental than a Confederate victory would have been. Even though such a victory would have dealt a death blow to the nation and a devastating blow to the cause of self-government, it is true enough that the failure of popular government is not exactly rare in the history of the world. Far from being "astounding," it is all too common. But a war fought between white citizens over the fate of Black slaves that leads to the emancipation of four million men, women, and children is something both "fundamental and astounding."[5] It was a result neither of the protagonists (that is, neither insurgents nor government) had in mind.

That does not mean, however, that no one had it in mind. The abolitionists not only "looked for" but forwarded just such a result. Welcoming the thunderbolt of war, Frederick Douglass was convinced that its target was slavery itself. Listen to his editorial "Nemesis" from May 1861:

> Slaveholders have in their madness invited armed abolition to march to the deliverance of the slave. They have furnished the occasion, and bound up the fate of the Republic and that of the slave in the same bundle, and the one and the other must survive or perish together. Any attempt now to separate the freedom of the slave from the victory of the Government over slaveholding rebels and traitors; any attempt to secure peace to the whites while leaving the blacks in chains; any attempt to heal the wounds of the Republic, while the deadly virus of slavery is left to poison the blood, will be labor lost. The American people and the Government at Washington may refuse to recognize it for a time; but the "inexorable logic of events" will force it upon them in the end; that the war now being waged in this land is a war for and against slavery; and that it can never be effectually put down till one or the other of these vital forces is completely destroyed. The irrepressible conflict, long confined to words and votes, is now to be carried by bayonets and bullets, and may God defend the right!

THE GOD OF BATTLES

Halfway through the third paragraph, Lincoln dramatically shifts to the present tense, as he introduces yet another similarity: "Both read the same Bible, and pray to the same God; and each invokes His aid against the other." With their expectations and calculations foiled, both sides seek Divine assistance. They turn to the identical Bible, the identical God, and even the identical prayer. Their shared religiosity is the last commonality that Lincoln mentions in this sequence of five independent clauses, over four sentences, each beginning with an impartial, indefinite pronoun: "Neither . . . Neither . . . Each . . . Both . . . ; and each . . ." The bond of Christian belief has been weaponized, equally, by the parties to the war. They have deployed religion divisively, attempting to range God on their side.

From this point forward—approximately the halfway point of the speech—religion will be the main topic. This "same God" will be invoked a total of fourteen times over the next nine sentences. Beginning from the conflictual way that religious appeals have figured in the war, Lincoln will try to reverse this partisan appropriation of divine power. He does so not by insisting on a strict separation of religion and politics but rather by doing religion differently. God may be the God of Battles, but not in the sense traditionally understood and invoked.

Perhaps in imitation of the religious crusaders, Lincoln's own impartiality seems to break down in the next sentence. He bursts out: "It may seem strange that any men should dare to ask a just God's assistance in wringing their bread from the sweat of other men's faces." With this allusion to Genesis 3:19, Lincoln shows that he is one of the Bible readers. However, as so often with his recurrence to the Good Book, he repurposes the verse. Genesis 3:19 describes the curse of Adam, punished for his disobedience to God: "In the sweat of thy face shalt thou eat bread." Lincoln, in line with his Free Labor philosophy, suggests that the wrong of slavery lies in trying to shift that penalty of sweat onto others. The masters deny that they are sons of toil. Near the conclusion of the Lincoln–Douglas debates, Lincoln epitomized the essence of tyranny in one sentence: "You work and toil and earn bread, and I'll eat it." By contrast, liberty requires each to labor for himself and allows each to enjoy the fruit of that labor. In his speech on the *Dred Scott* decision, Lincoln had offered a Black woman as his paradigmatic example of this universal truth: "in her natural right to eat the bread she earns with her own hands without asking leave of any one else, she is my equal, and the equal of all others." So long as the sweat is honest, Lincoln suggests that Adam's punishment is as much blessing as curse.

Opposed to the tyrannical principle is "the common right of humanity," which Lincoln, in his 1859 address at the Wisconsin state fair, described as "the just and generous and prosperous system which opens the way for all, gives hope to all, and energy and progress and improvement of condition to all." The very structure of our physical being, Lincoln argued, accords with this Free Labor conception of political economy. Noting in that same speech that "the Author of man" made each of us with one head, one mouth, and one pair of hands, Lincoln surmised that the parts of the individual whole were meant to "co-operate": "each head is the natural guardian, director and protector of the hands and mouth inseparably connected with it." This is not, however, an individualism that disassociates from others, leaving nothing for the body politic to do. Indeed, Lincoln's exposition of the Free Labor (or self-ownership) theory concludes with this strong policy deduction: "and that being so, every head should be cultivated and improved, by whatever will add to its capacity for performing its charge. In one word, free labor insists on universal education." In his promotion of education, Lincoln goes so far as to say that it isn't just the fruits of toil that are sustaining and sweet; rather, toil itself "lightens and sweetens" by being combined with "cultivated thought." No labor is purely manual when undertaken freely by an observing, discovering, inventing human being.

Lincoln's references to bread, toil, and sweat in the Second Inaugural are the fruit of his own well-developed thought on the significance of human labor, not only in its economic dimension but psychically or holistically considered. The companion piece to the Address to the Wisconsin State Agricultural Society is the Lecture on Discoveries and Inventions, also delivered in the period between Lincoln's loss to Douglas in the senatorial contest of 1858 and what was, in effect, the launch of his presidential bid in the Cooper Union Address of 1860. In examining the difference between slave labor and free labor, both speeches connect that difference to education. The call for "universal education" made to the farmers at the fair takes a more historical and high-toned form in the Lecture on Discoveries and Inventions, where Lincoln describes the invention of the printing press as having emancipated the mind from its enslavement to a "false and under estimate of itself." The political aim of "rising to equality" depends on the advance of literacy.

While the Second Inaugural does not set forth governmental policy, the searing critique that Lincoln presents of the essence of slavery—commodifying human beings and reducing them to beasts of burden—hints at the policies to come. Figuring out Lincoln's plans for reconstruction is not sheer speculation. Consider the elements featured in his last public speech, five weeks after the inauguration and four days before his death. When praising the new "free-state constitution" of Louisiana, Lincoln highlighted two measures: "giving the benefit of public schools equally to black and white, and empowering the Legislature to confer the elective franchise upon the colored man." Although there was dissatisfaction among the radical Republicans that the postwar Louisiana constitution did not directly and fully extend the franchise, Lincoln argued for accepting this start, as "the egg" to "the fowl," inasmuch as "we shall sooner have the fowl by hatching the egg than by smashing it." Certainly, Lincoln did not slight the value of the franchise—and the qualified franchise he recommended was but a first step toward a full realization of the consent principle. Nonetheless, I believe he regarded the educational provision as the most urgent and vital. Education is the steady drumbeat in his public statements, going all the way back to his first declaration of candidacy in 1832, when he declared that education was "the most important subject which we as a people can be engaged in."

The Louisiana constitution's attention to public schooling without regard to race leads Lincoln to deliver the most heartening line in the April 1865 address: "The colored man too, in seeing **all united for him**, is inspired with vigilance, and energy, and daring." Blacks are not only to join the American collective, but the "all" is now to show itself united "for him," which is to say united in his interest and to his good, thereby encouraging his own determined self-effort. Lincoln's adjectives—vigilance, energy, and daring—welcome African American achievement and assertiveness. At the same time, the word "vigilance" indicates Lincoln's awareness that Blacks in particular will need to be alert to the continued presence and resurgence of the tyrannical spirit of "crowned kings, money kings, and land kings."

Having strongly expressed his conviction that slavery is at odds with God's justice (and having implied that justice is His prime attribute), Lincoln then pulls back from his assignment of moral blame. To execute this *volte-face*, he paraphrases another Bible verse (Matthew 7:1): "but let us judge not that we be not judged." He puts these two opposed thoughts, each drawn directly from the Bible, into one sentence. God is anti-slavery; but God also warns against the exercise of human judgment. Human beings should beware of hypocrisy. All are sinners and guilty. The juxtaposition administers a check to self-righteousness, especially on the anti-slavery side. This is his first use of the words "us" and "we"—and they entail a correction of his own side in the struggle. Lincoln takes the general order of Matthew 7:1—"Judge not, that **ye** be not judged"—and applies it to "us," the opponents of slavery. The temptation to denounce the other side is strong and a love of justice encourages righteous anger. Lincoln briefly gives vent to such feelings but then reins "us" in with a reminder that "we," too, are under judgment. Yet it is worth remembering that Lincoln was a wily courtroom lawyer. Even when an attorney's line of attack is successfully challenged and the objection sustained, the jury may have trouble ignoring, despite the judge's instruction to do so, what was let slip. Lincoln's New Testament injunction does not retract his Old Testament expression of righteous anger. Both remain in the mind, balanced and in tension.

Lincoln returns to the fact that both sides pray. Taking to heart the warning against disparaging the content of another person's prayers, Lincoln has a new thought. Since prayers are addressed to a higher power, perhaps we can conclude something about God's judgment from His answers to prayer. The analysis of the evidence is logical: Since the prayers of the two parties are diametrically opposed, the prayers of both cannot be answered. God himself is bound by the principle of non-contradiction—"God cannot be for and against the same thing at the same time," as Lincoln had explicitly stated in his 1862 Meditation on the Divine Will, a remarkable fragment that presents Lincoln's preliminary thinking-through of the argument of the Second Inaugural. Then he observes, "that of neither has been answered fully." This extension of the thought is curious, since one of the logical possibilities is that God favored one side's prayers over the other, as God did in that original fratricidal conflict when Abel's offering saw favor and Cain's did not. Isn't the progress of Union arms, mentioned in the opening paragraph, a sign that God is on the Union side? Lincoln, however, leaves out this possibility. He doesn't make the usual triumphalist move—a move that was being made at the time by many religious leaders throughout the North. Instead he administers another check to moral superiority, saying modestly that the prayer of neither side has been answered fully. That is certainly true of the insurgents; they can't be too impressed with the efficacy of prayer at this late date in the war. Lincoln's phrasing covers over the significant gap between the outcomes for the two parties. The

Union may not have gotten all it wanted, but it is on the cusp of winning. Lincoln's formulation draws attention away from that fact. He emphasizes, instead, the commonality of disappointed prayers—years' worth of them, as the war dragged on and on and hundreds of thousands of young men died.

THE ALL AND THE ALMIGHTY

How to explain these unanswered prayers? In the pivotal sentence of the speech, Lincoln posits: "The Almighty has His own purposes." Before proceeding, we must admit that there is an alternative explanation. Perhaps the prayers of all go unanswered because there is no One listening. Just as Lincoln said, "And the war came," he could have said, "And the war continues." This result, although undesired, might be the product of the inexorable logic of cause and effect. Lincoln, however, either rejects or suppresses this atheistic possibility. Nonetheless, he was aware that events could be read this way, as indicated in the letter to Thurlow Weed that he wrote a week or so after the Second Inaugural. Noting that reaction to the speech had not been positive, Lincoln explained why: "Men are not flattered by being shown that there has been a difference of purpose between the Almighty and them. To deny it, however, in this case, is to deny that there is a God governing the world."

Scholars have long disputed the status of Lincoln's faith. There is evidence of his early and thoroughgoing religious skepticism, but also plenty of later evidence of a maturing religious sensibility and perhaps deep conviction. Fortunately, studying the Second Inaugural does not require settling the matter of his personal belief. The purpose of his speaking is, at all times (with the possible exception of his poetry), not self-expression but rather political persuasion, availing himself of the subtleties of that art, without sacrifice of honest purpose. Moreover, he has the rhetorical luxury—a luxury lost to politicians today—of taking faith for granted. His listeners are overwhelmingly "believers in a Living God."

Assuming Americans' belief in the divinity, Lincoln can flip the perspective of his audience from their human purposes, on view in their prayers, to God's higher purposes—or rather to speculation about His purposes. God is not our tool or instrument; we are His "human instrumentalities," the term Lincoln used in his Meditation on the Divine Will. God is more than "a just God" whose assistance can be sought. He is the All-Mighty. Omnipotence is another divine attribute. Yet, all-powerful does not mean free from obscurity. Mysterious have been the purposes to which His power has been put. Lincoln hints, however, that the terrible and protracted course of the war, as well as its fundamental and astounding result, must be part of the Almighty's plan. God's intention has disclosed itself slowly and through our mutual suffering, through the "woe" we have undergone. Lincoln quotes another Bible verse, Matthew 18:7, this time accurately and in full: "Woe unto the world because of offences! for it must needs be that offences come; but woe to that man by whom the offence cometh!" The verse is a powerful reminder of man's sinfulness and its wages. A fallen or selfish nature endowed with free will is a guarantee of wrongdoing. The resulting "woe" is two-fold; "the world" suffers from the wrong and the wrongdoer suffers God's wrath.

After reminding his audience of these tenets of the faith,

Lincoln arrives at the point toward which the analysis has been aiming:

> If we shall suppose that American Slavery is one of those offences which, in the providence of God, must needs come, but which, having continued through His appointed time, He now wills to remove, and that He gives to both North and South, this terrible war, as the woe due to those by whom the offence came, shall we discern therein any departure from those divine attributes which the believers in a Living God always ascribe to Him?

In this, the longest sentence of the speech, Lincoln presents a theological interpretation of the meaning of the Civil War. Simply put, the war is the blood price the nation must pay for the sin of slavery. Note that this interpretation is presented not as certain knowledge or doctrine but as a supposition: "If we shall suppose . . ." The interpretation is a hypothesis, offered as such. The diffidence with which it is offered and the complexity of the sentence itself drain away any of the fanaticism that is so worrisome when religion seeps into politics. While using religion for political purposes, Lincoln does so to encourage humility rather than pride or certainty.

Another thing to note is that the word "slavery" finally appears. Slavery is not Southern slavery or African slavery but "American Slavery," with each word capitalized. Because the offense of slavery belongs to the nation, the punishment is meted out to both North and South. All citizens have been complicit in slavery. Even those who opposed it could be said to have benefited from it. All Americans wore cotton and consumed sugar. Many northerners made fortunes (or inherited fortunes) from the trade in those goods and the trade in slaves themselves. In a way, Lincoln is describing what is today called "white privilege"—the unmerited status and advantages that accrue based on the possession of white skin and built on the oppression of those of another skin color. Perhaps a caveat is in order, however, since Lincoln actually does not speak, as we so frequently do, in racialized terms. If cotton-wearing constitutes complicity, then free Blacks (and one in ten people of color were free) received the privilege as well. Of course, free Blacks suffered many forms of economic and civic exclusion, but there was discrimination against segments of the white population as well ("No Irish Need Apply"). In other words, the notion of "white privilege" is both too narrow and too broad. Lincoln's strategy is to nationalize the wrong, insisting it is "American Slavery," rather than to racialize it. The collective that must admit wrong is the nation itself.

Having framed his hypothesis, Lincoln then, still in the same sentence, follows with a question. If the supposition of God punishing the nation for American Slavery is true, then would "we discern therein any departure from those divine attributes which the believers in a Living God always ascribe to Him?" The implied answer is "no." A God who acts in this way would be a just God—all-powerful and providential. Lincoln's mention of "the providence of God" points to two further divine attributes: His omniscience and His active, loving care. God's providence requires that He see the future and that all lives matter to Him. The sentence concludes with yet another divine descriptor, the most evocative of the speech: "a Living God." Lincoln capitalized neither "just" (in "a just God") nor "providence" (in "the providence of God") but he does capitalize "Living," even though the King James Bible, which contains more than two dozen references to the "living God," nowhere capitalizes this adjective. The phrase appears in various contexts, often in relation to national transgression and punishment. Perhaps in Lincoln's mind was Jeremiah 10:10: "But the LORD *is* the true God, he *is* the living God, and an everlasting king: at his wrath the earth shall tremble, and the nations shall not be able to abide his indignation." Or the similar sentiment of Hebrews 10:30–31: "For we know him that hath said, Vengeance *belongeth* unto me, I will recompense, saith the Lord. And again, The Lord shall judge his people. *It is* a fearful thing to fall into the hands of the living God." This "terrible war," with all its death and destruction, is the deed of the Living God—or at least thinking so is not at odds with a Christian conception of the Divine.

Yet, we might raise some questions about this implied answer regarding God's justice. Is it just for hundreds of thousands of non-slaveholders to die in the conflict? All the Union dead were non-slaveholders and many of them were determined foes of slavery. Moreover, a significant number were former slaves who, after the Emancipation Proclamation, fought on the Union side. Even most of the southern deaths were of non-slaveholders, since slaveholders (especially those with large numbers of slaves) were a tiny minority. There's a case to be made that the poor whites of the South were victims of the oligarchic slave-ocracy, too. Although their oppression obviously differed in type and degree from that of the slaves, nonetheless the great majority of whites were impoverished by the absence of a Free Labor system in the South; they took refuge in the psychological com-

pensation of white supremacy (a form of co-optation that was
deliberately crafted and manipulated by the ruling few).

We might also raise the question of generational fairness.
In what sense was the war the just deserts—the woe due—to
this particular generation of Americans? This might be "His appointed time" for vengeance, but why should all those previous
generations, some of whom began the offense, get off scot-free
(in this world at least)? Is collective guilt a just concept? The ordinances given in Deuteronomy governing human justice make
clear that "The fathers shall not be put to death for the children,
neither shall the children be put to death for the fathers: every
man shall be put to death for his own sin" (Deuteronomy 24:16).
God's justice (or even justice among nations) may be different.
Avoiding bald assertion, Lincoln merely floats this interpretation of the war as a hypothesis and a question. Furthermore,
he ascribes the attributes of God to the ascriptions of "the believers," without indicating that he is one of them. The "we"
of this sentence cannot be co-extensive with "the believers." If
nothing else, the category of believers is larger, not being limited temporally or geographically to the United States. Thus, in
one sense, the "we" is narrower. The "we" are those who hear
Lincoln's hypothesis and try to "discern" the answer to his question as to whether God, on an orthodox understanding, would
act this way. In another sense, though, the "we" is more capa-
cious since it must include both believers and some number of
non-believers. Remarkably, given the way Lincoln has framed
the premise of his question, both groups would be forced to
give the same answer. Lincoln hopes that Americans will be inclined not only to see no "departure" from Bible-based notions

of the divinity, but to accept the interpretation—supposition and all—as true.

This sentence has been intensely demanding. Before he continues his account of God's retributive purpose in the third paragraph's final sentence, Lincoln interjects a digression. He expresses our human reaction to this "mighty scourge of war." We hope and pray for it to cease. The just penalty is more than we can take. The sentence rhymes and its ease of expression serves as a breather between the two flanking sentences, both of which are complex in construction and painful in content. But this little stanza—

> Fondly do we hope,
> fervently do we pray,
> That this mighty scourge of war
> may speedily pass away

—offers more than a moment's respite. It brings the prayers of the nation to a new place. Prayer was first introduced allusively back in the second paragraph through the word "deprecate." Etymologically, "deprecate" means to avert by prayer. Lincoln had said that "Both parties deprecated war." Once the war came, however, both parties moved from praying to avert war to praying for victory in war. Now, however, in his final exploration of prayer and its efficacy, Lincoln presents both sides praying that the war, understood as a shared and deserved woe—a scourging, a whipping—will cease. The prayers of the nation have converged on the longing for divine mercy. But just as the earlier prayers were not fully answered, this prayer for mercy might not be, either. God's will is what will prevail.

DIVINE REPARATIONS

To finish the third paragraph, Lincoln formulates another hypothetical about God's will—one that envisions the full scale of eye-for-eye divine reparations. An angry God might require the war's continuance "until all the wealth piled by the bond-man's two hundred and fifty years of unrequited toil shall be sunk, and until every drop of blood drawn with the lash, shall be paid by another drawn with the sword." Lincoln invites his audience to contemplate how much the slaves contributed to the building of the continent. Note that he uses an old English term, "bond-man," a term that highlights personhood; this wealth was created by human beings bound in servitude. The term has Biblical resonance also; it is used repeatedly in the King James version of Deuteronomy to remind the Hebrews of their deliverance: "But thou shalt remember that thou wast a bondman in Egypt, and the LORD thy God redeemed thee thence" (Deuteronomy 24:18). If Blacks are analogous to the children of Israel, then the United States is the Pharaoh, whom God smites. Lincoln had warned of this parallel between American and "Egyptian bondage" once before, at the conclusion of his *Dred Scott* speech.

But more than wealth must be recompensed. The only way to extract labor from someone not laboring by contract is by the lash. Lincoln had seen its operation, not often but enough. Much contemporary radical thought about race is framed around "the Black body" and the array of assaults upon it, beginning with such lashes. While the aim of "engaged scholarship" is to document and resist this violent objectification, there is something dangerously reductive in the language. Constant talk of "the Black body" risks engraining the whip-holder's view that all he deals with is a body, rather than an ensouled body (or better yet, an embodied soul). Contemporary radicalism, mirroring the wider culture, has lost sight of the spirit. Lincoln's formulation is better. He speaks of "blood," the life force. The earliest references to blood in Genesis 4:10 tell of God's reaction to Cain's fratricide: "And he said, What hast thou done? The voice of thy brother's blood crieth unto me from the ground." The shedding of blood is fundamentally not an assault on a body but on a being made in the image of God.[6] According to Lincoln, God might well avenge "every drop of blood."

The earlier mention of the war as a "scourge" is now tied to the literal scourge of the "lash." This war between brothers, North and South, is divine chastisement for the other brothers'—the Black brothers—enslavement. How much blood would have to be drawn for the scourge of the sword to equal the scourge of the lash? The answer depends on how long the lash has been plied. In this, the penultimate sentence of the address, Lincoln goes back to the origin date of American Slavery in the Jamestown colony.[7] Subtracting 250 years from 1865 places us at 1615. Lincoln's approximate date is not far off the actual date of 1619.

Presumably Lincoln's source was the historian William Grimshaw, whom he had read in his youth. In a section of Grimshaw's *History of the United States* covering the years 1616 through 1619, Grimshaw describes captives "from the coast of Guinea" arriving on a "Dutch ship" and being sold to the Virginia planters. Although not providing a precise date, he does highlight both the far-reaching effects of this event and its immorality: "What a climax of human cupidity and turpitude; what a glaring inconsistency between the public professions, and the private actions, of individuals, are here presented for consideration!" Grimshaw concludes his history with an account of the progress of gradual emancipation in all the northern states and a plea to end domestic bondage in the remaining states, citing the words of the Declaration and the instruction of George Washington.

In setting this baseline for American Slavery, Lincoln incorporates more than a century and a half of enslavement predating the era of the Revolution and the Constitution. It is as if the United States, at its creation, assumed that colonial debt. Throughout the 1850s, Lincoln consistently argued that political necessity left the founders no choice but to accommodate the pre-existing colonial injustice, even as they pronounced it a grievous wrong. Thus, his 1858 speech at Chicago explained the compromises of the Constitution by saying: "we could not secure the good we did secure if we grasped for more." The plea of necessity not only explains, but even excuses, since "to the extent that a necessity is imposed upon a man he must submit to it." However, here in the Second Inaugural, Lincoln adds the somber thought that submission to necessity does not negate the weight of the past and its moral obligation. Equivalence would have to account for the spilled blood and stolen wealth not only of the slaves then living, but that of the total number of persons enslaved in North America from 1619 to 1865.

The long timeframe of American Slavery has been much in the news of late, partly because of the recent quadricentennial and, probably more lastingly, as a result of the 1619 Project of the *New York Times,* which seeks to re-center our national self-understanding on this date and its perduring legacy, with a view to an ideologically leftist recasting of American laws and institutions. Yet it is worth pointing out that awareness of the significance of 1619 is nothing new. Through Lincoln's reference to "the bond-man's two hundred and fifty years of unrequited toil," 1619 is the featured date in one of the best known and most revered of American speeches. What is new about the recent 1619 Project is the attack on 1776, 1787, and even 1865. The 1619 Project argues that the nation is irredeemably racist, racist from the beginning and racist throughout—structurally racist. Lincoln disagrees. 1776 was not a continuation of the spirit of 1619 but its antithesis.

1787, too, although pragmatic in its compromises, was anti-slavery in principle. It was the Confederate constitution of 1861 that enshrined the spirit of 1619, as a quick comparison between the two documents reveals. In the U.S. Constitution, neither "slave" nor "slavery" appears. In the three clauses that are generally understood to have reference to the institution (Article 1, sections 2 and 9, and Article 4, section 2), those affected are unambiguously referred to as "persons." Moreover, the intention of two of those clauses was arguably anti-slavery, inasmuch as the first one lessened by two-fifths the electoral weight of the slaveholding states in the House of Representatives and the second made possible Congress's abolition of the international slave trade in 1808, in the belief (mistaken it turned out) that choking off the supply would suffocate the institution of slavery. Of course, as compromises, these provisions can be viewed from the reverse perspective, with the three-fifths clause augmenting the slaveholding "interest" by three-fifths and the importation clause granting a twenty-year reprieve to the international slave trade during which time the total number of slaves increased substantially. Yet however one construes these particular clauses (whether as penalties imposed on slaveholding or concessions to it), the language of the document is free of invidious discrimination and explicit racism. By contrast, the Constitution of the Confederate States speaks repeatedly of "slaves" and "negroes of the African race" and never of "persons," further specifying that "No . . . law denying or impairing the right of property in negro slaves shall be passed" and that in the "new territory" that the Confederacy might acquire "the institution of negro slavery, as it now exists in the Confederate States, shall be recognized and protected by Congress and by the Territorial government."

Despite postwar diversionary blather about "states' rights" from "Lost Cause" advocates, the Confederate constitution federalized or nationalized slavery in a way that the U.S. Constitution never did. As Alexander Stephens, vice president of the Confederacy, affirmed, slavery was the "corner-stone" of their new edifice. In considering the relation of 1619 to 1776/1787, all Americans should remember what Stephens proclaimed:

> The prevailing ideas entertained by [Thomas Jefferson] and most of the leading statesmen at the time of the formation of the old constitution, were that the enslavement of the African was in violation of the laws of nature; that it was wrong in principle, socially, morally, and politically. It was an evil they knew not well how to deal with, but the general opinion of the men of that day was that, somehow or other in the order of Providence, the institution would be evanescent and pass away. . . . Those ideas, however, were fundamentally wrong. They rested upon the assumption of the equality of races. . . . Our new government is founded upon exactly the opposite idea; its foundations are laid, its corner-stone rests, upon the great truth that the negro is not equal to the white man; that slavery—subordination to the superior race—is his

natural and normal condition. This, our new government, is
the first, in the history of the world, based upon this great
physical, philosophical, and moral truth.

The protection of the Confederacy's expanding slave empire required that the original non-racist charters be forsworn.

A few additional data points might help in understanding the
significance of 1619 and its relation to the timing of the eventual national rupture. We should never forget that the enslavement of Africans was a global phenomenon. The Arab-Muslim
slave trade to the East was in existence ten centuries before the
Atlantic trade began and was more extensive in every respect
(although hard numbers are hard to come by). On the western
side, the Trans-Atlantic Slave Trade Database estimates there
were 12.5 million Africans transported to the New World, with
10.7 million surviving the Middle Passage. Of those 10.7 million, only 388,000 (3.6 percent) landed in North America. South
America and the Caribbean were the favored destinations for
the Atlantic slave trade. From those small beginnings, it took almost two centuries, until 1810, for the total number of enslaved
persons in the United States to reach one million. But over the
next forty years, from 1810 to 1860, the slave population, now
concentrated exclusively in half the states, went from one million to four million. Slavery in North America, despite its colonial origins, was indeed American Slavery. The total number of
enslaved persons from 1619 to 1865 is estimated at five million.
Astonishingly, that means that roughly 80 percent of the enslaved persons who ever resided in North America were alive in
1865. But that also means that 80 percent of those ever enslaved
in North America were freed in consequence of the Civil War.

One soldier died for every seven persons enslaved from 1619 to 1865; and one soldier died for every six persons freed by the 13th Amendment.

Returning to Lincoln, we see how understanding our history aright requires taking proper account of these various dates and their true relationship. Lincoln reads our national story as a struggle between the principles of natural right, enshrined in the Declaration and the Constitution, and the violation of those principles in American Slavery, beginning in 1619 and spiraling down to its nadir in 1861. In the Second Inaugural, Lincoln makes God himself the vindicator and upholder of those principles of right.

Although the bloodletting had already been extensive, it might continue until God is satisfied. If so, what follows? Lincoln does not conclude by calling for national repentance; perhaps that would cross a theological-political bright line of sorts. Instead, as he did earlier, he shifts to our judgment of God's judgment. Before, he argued that if God is punishing us, then wouldn't we have to say He is doing the God-like thing? Now, he argues that if God keeps punishing us, then "as was said three thousand years ago, so still it must be said 'the judgments of the Lord, are true and righteous altogether.'" This final quotation is of Psalms 19:9 and it takes us back even further into the past, well beyond the 250 years of American Slavery. Scholars date this Psalm to 1015 B.C. Lincoln's chronology—"as was said three thousand years ago"—is again basically accurate. Lincoln has re-situated the civil conflict of 1861 through 1865 within the wider horizon inaugurated by the events of 1619 and then re-situated that historic wrong within the widest imaginable horizon, beginning from the expulsion from Eden. His four direct quotes from the Bible (Genesis 3:19, Matthew 7:1, Matthew 18:7, and Psalms 19:9) sketch a way of thinking about offense and judgment.

THE MORAL PREREQUISITES FOR RECONSTRUCTION

What does Lincoln's interpretation achieve? As I read it, it makes possible the final paragraph of the speech. If Americans will join in understanding the war in this way, then space will be cleared for human charity, or at least a lessening of human malice. In other words, Lincoln's theological interpretation has a political postwar purpose.

Foresight is the statesman's special gift. Lincoln clearly saw the obstacles ahead, the first of which was northern arrogance. Many commentators have noted how the Second Inaugural constituted a reproof to those, like Congressman Thaddeus Stevens, who thought the South should be treated as "conquered provinces" and made "to eat the fruit of foul rebellion." Vindictiveness was perfectly understandable; after all, secession was treason, capitally punishable. Individuals could have been forced to pay "the hemp tax" (Daniel Webster's clever term for hanging for treason, from his Second Reply to Hayne), and the seceded states could have been reduced to territorial status. By shifting the focus from secession to slavery and then insisting on the complicity of both North and South in American Slavery, Lincoln tries to defuse that moralistic anger. Although not mentioning the abolitionists, he echoes certain of their themes; they had long been denouncing slavery and slaveholders as an offense against God and man. Lincoln adopts the biblical language of "offense" but drops the thundering tones of anathema. Humbly, he asks each American to consider whether God isn't being just. That leading question should lessen prosecutorial zeal.

Lincoln saw dangers—likely more intractable—on the southern side as well. He did not want to aggravate the inevitable feelings of sectional resentment. Since northern triumphalism would only exacerbate Lost Cause romanticism, Lincoln's reproof to the North is at the same time part of his olive branch to the South. Note that he is not displaying magnanimity toward the defeated. Rather than assume the stance of a generous victor, Lincoln does something more radical. In the Second Inaugural, he refuses to call the result of the war a victory for the Union. The emphasis is instead on shared national suffering as a consequence of shared national transgression. Convincing southerners would be difficult. Already southern theologians were explaining the Confederate loss as providential in the sense that God often tests his chosen people. They were not inclined to read the war as chastisement for their way of life. Nonetheless, by generalizing the blame for slavery to the entire nation, Lincoln does what he can to help southerners admit their error. Only if the South were prepared to acknowledge the offense could a better and smoother post-slavery path be opened.

Finally, Lincoln was concerned about not only relations between the sections but relations between the races. There was imminent danger of white resistance to Black freedom and Black advancement. There was also a danger of retaliation and vengeance on the part of the freed people, both for the wrong of slavery and the wrongs that would continue to be perpetrated. Obviously, one speech is not going to put race relations on a new footing. Nonetheless, Lincoln's explanation of the war seeks to bridge the racial divide.

In no uncertain terms, whites are told that God was all along on the side of the bondsmen. This was not a new thought or a new rhetorical strategy. In Query 18 of his *Notes on the State of Virginia*, Thomas Jefferson had tried to frighten his fellow slaveholders into considering gradual emancipation by reminding them of God's sympathies. "I tremble for my country," he said, "when I reflect that God is just: that his justice cannot sleep for ever." Envisioning a possible slave insurrection, Jefferson declared, "The Almighty has no attribute which can take side with us in such a contest." Lincoln is revisiting this famous statement of Jefferson's, echoing its invocation of "The Almighty" and His "attributes." Rather than the servile war that Jefferson feared, the moment of reckoning took the form of civil war. Yet, race war initiated by disgruntled whites might still break out. Lincoln's interpretation fortifies the nation to resist such revanchism.

Fostering an enlightened public opinion that could resist rearguard actions was important, but a sentiment of national contrition could also support bold steps forward. Frederick Douglass certainly saw the political advantages of penitence, even if it proved an all-too-temporary mood. In January 1865, in a speech entitled "What the Black Man Wants," he observed, "We all feel, in the existence of this Rebellion, that judgments terrible, wide-spread, far-reaching, overwhelming, are abroad in the land; and we feel, in view of these judgments, just now, a disposition to learn righteousness. This is the hour." Believing there was only a narrow window provided by "the chastisement of this Rebellion," Douglass pressed for adoption of the 15th Amendment. Although he knew that the guarantees might not be honored, it was still imperative to get nonracial citizenship and suffrage enshrined in the Constitution. The postwar amendments would set the standard, thus providing a weapon for the future. Whether Lincoln would have shifted from his cautious endorsement of a qualified suffrage to universal suffrage cannot be known, but, like Douglass, he was leveraging "white guilt" for reformative political purposes.

What, then, does this interpretation offer the freedmen? It confirms that God has been on their side, despite taking so long to vindicate them. Judged from the human perspective, justice delayed is justice denied. Yet, as with the Israelites, somehow the delay is to be understood as in accord with "His appointed time." Beyond that painful lesson in patience, the American president has just implied that God would be justified in exacting eye-for-eye vengeance on their behalf. Some commentators have been appalled at the bloodthirstiness of this vision. Richard Brookhiser, for instance, in *Founders' Son*, pronounced the "moral calculus" of this "eloquent, disturbing, wrongheaded speech" to be "outrageous." Whether it is or not, I believe this portrayal of divine reparations is part of what is offered to African Americans. While the national confession of guilt does not do away with the need for civic justice going forward, the thought that America has been punished, really punished, might incline these new citizens toward a stance of thanksgiving for what Frederick Douglass, in his Oration in Memory of Abraham Lincoln, called "our blood-bought freedom" and patient resolve for the struggles to come. Moreover, if full justice was not exacted by God— for, in the final analysis, God was merciful to the nation—then African Americans should accept and imitate that generosity.

Just to be clear, leaving vengeance to the Lord does not mean Lincoln was counseling Blacks to be politically quiescent. He had already done the opposite in the Emancipation Proclamation, where for the first time in a state paper, an American president directly addressed the Black population, issuing first an injunction, then an invitation. Already worried about racial conflict, Lincoln warns, "And I hereby enjoin upon the people so declared to be free to abstain from all violence," but then he adds the qualifier, "unless in necessary self-defence." That is a most significant exception. It acknowledges that southern whites might be the beginners of a race war, just as they had been the beginners of the sectional war. In effect, Lincoln puts whites on notice that Blacks have an inalienable right to life and liberty that they themselves may vindicate should police protection fail them. Lincoln then goes on to welcome African Americans into the military service of the United States, unfettering the "sable arm" as Frederick Douglass and others had been urging. Thus, Lincoln's counsel of non-violence is sufficiently flexible to allow Blacks to respond with "well-poised bayonet," in individual self-defense and in defense of the nation.

Frederick Douglass seemed to understand what Lincoln was aiming to achieve with his Second Inaugural Address. "More vital substance than I have ever seen compressed in a space so narrow," was his assessment in *Life and Times*, the final iteration of his autobiography. Perhaps his verdict was influenced by a personal consideration. Many have told the story (and none so well as Douglass himself) of his attendance at the inauguration and the White House reception afterward, where it required Lincoln's intervention to ensure he was admitted. Once inside, Douglass was greeted by Lincoln with the assurance that "there is no man in the country whose opinion I value more than yours. I want to know what you think of it?" Douglass's response—"Mr. Lincoln, that was a sacred effort"—insightfully subsumed the theological or "sacred" dimension of the speech to its political purpose. That is to say, he rightly understood the speech as an "effort" to effect the fullest national and racial reconciliation. For the next three decades, on nearly every subsequent occasion that he mentioned Abraham Lincoln, Frederick Douglass quoted the divine reparations sentence from the Second Inaugural. One can only imagine with what depth of feeling, since he had experienced the scourging of the lash and had lived to see his sons, Charles Remond and Lewis Henry, enlist in the 54th Massachusetts, wielding the sword.

LET US STRIVE ON

Lincoln's spiritualized interpretation of the war enables the various parties to rise above their worst passions, thus restoring equanimity and clearing the path for better forms of human action. The one-sentence concluding paragraph describes those transcendent actions. The core of the sentence is an imperative: "Let us strive on." The essential demand that Lincoln makes of the people is modified with three clauses before and four after. The three preceding the demand—"with malice toward none; with charity for all; with firmness in the right, as God gives us to see the right"—explain how or in what spirit we should strive. The four after—"to finish the work we are in; to bind up the nation's wounds; to care for him who shall have borne the battle, and for his widow, and his orphan—to do all which may achieve and cherish a just, and a lasting peace, among ourselves, and with all nations"—explain what we should strive for. The aim of the speech has been to arrive at this call to action.

The order of the modifiers is deliberate. Before charity is possible, malice must be overcome. Even if the virtue of charity can't quite be reached, avoiding malice would be no mean accomplishment. In an 1862 letter to Cuthbert Bullitt, defending his all-out prosecution of the war as dutiful, Lincoln had pledged, "I shall do nothing in malice. What I deal with is too vast for malicious dealing." At the same time, Lincoln was aware of the malice of others. On two important occasions, one a state paper, the other a public letter, he had branded white prejudice as "malicious" and "malignant." In his 1862 Annual Message to Congress, Lincoln spoke against white resistance to "free colored persons remaining in the country." Even while continuing to see some value in colonization (should the freed people be interested), he denounced those whites who feared labor competition with Blacks, post-slavery, calling their objection "largely imaginary, if not sometimes malicious."

A few months later, Lincoln penned a public letter to James C. Conkling, addressing Democratic Unionists who were still unhappy with the Emancipation Proclamation. Gone now is any talk of colonization. Instead, Lincoln describes the Black warriors as vindicators of the principle of the ballot, thus preparing public opinion for the Black claim to that ballot. As he celebrates the contribution of "black men" who "have helped mankind on to this great consummation," Lincoln refers to those "white ones" (he doesn't seem to want to call them "men" even) "with malignant heart" who "have strove to hinder it." Lincoln effectively shames the regressive striving of the white supremacists, which is the opposite of the Second Inaugural's "let us strive on." The great popularity achieved by the Conkling letter suggests that Lincoln, in concert with 180,000 Black troops, was having some success in addressing the problem of anti-Black animus among white Americans.

While the Bible certainly denounces malice (as in Ephesians 4:31: "Let all bitterness, and wrath, and anger, and clamour, and evil speaking, be put away from you, with all malice"), charity is a more religiously freighted term, being one of the cardinal Christian virtues (1st Corinthians 13:13: "And now abideth faith, hope, charity, these three; but the greatest of these *is* charity"). Since the Lyceum Address, Lincoln had been appropriating religious language and attitudes for political purposes. In a fragment from 1858, Lincoln had attempted to hold Christians to their own highest values when he offered the following definition of charity: "'*Give* to him that is needy' is the Christian rule of charity; but 'Take from him that is needy' is the rule of slavery." In the Second Inaugural, however, charity does not mean the actual practice of charitable giving but rather a spirit of good will that should inform our civic striving. There may be times when that loving spirit requires the bestowal of benefits, but there may also be times when acting "with charity" might dictate stern treatment. After all, in laying out the requirements for a just war, Saint Augustine spoke of "benevolent harshness," prosecuting a war with love of the enemy in one's heart. Just as Lincoln sought to attach a spirit of reverence to the letter of the law, he seeks to imbue the demands of duty with an overarching spirit of kindness and patience. Lincoln's most extensive rumination on the spirit of charity came in his early Temperance Address, where he explained the reasons for the success of the Washingtonian temperance reformers (a society of former drinkers in the mode of Alcoholics Anonymous) as compared to the far less successful fire-and-brimstone variety (whose rhetoric mirrored that of the radical abolitionists):

> Benevolence and charity possess *their* hearts entirely; and out of the abundance of their hearts, their tongues give utterance. "Love through all their actions runs, and all their words are mild." In this spirit they speak and act, and in the same, they are heard and regarded. And when such is the temper of the advocate, and such of the audience, no good cause can be unsuccessful.

Neither in 1842 nor 1865 does Lincoln lessen his reliance on reason or recommend a purely emotive compassion. In the Temperance Address, he argues that professions of friendship for a man are "the great high road to his reason." In the Second Inaugural, Lincoln moves from charity to the need for the exercise of moral judgment; we must act "with firmness in the right," even if such firmness might look uncharitable. Think of Lincoln's refusal to pardon Nathaniel Gordon, the first and only slave trader ever hanged under American law. (The incident is well told by William Lee Miller in *President Lincoln: The Duty of a Statesman*.) Even though involvement in the banned international trade had been a capital crime since 1820, lax enforcement, acquittals, and commutations allowed violators to escape the penalty. Amid public petitions and protest rallies on Gordon's behalf, Lincoln held fast. Refusing to grant a pardon, he did, however, grant a two-week stay of execution to give the convicted pirate time for "the necessary preparation for the awful change which awaits him." Lincoln took the pedagogical liberty of indicating how he ought to spend that time:

> In granting this respite, it becomes my painful duty to ad-
> monish the prisoner that, relinquishing all expectation of
> pardon by Human Authority, he refer himself alone to the
> mercy of the common God and Father of all men.

There were 897 Africans found below decks on the last of the many slave ships Nathaniel Gordon captained. Lincoln implies that the "common God and Father of all men" might not be any more inclined to mercy in this case than was Lincoln himself.

Just as charity is guided by moral firmness, that firmness is balanced by the insight that we are fallible creatures. God gives us some degree of moral vision, but as the previous paragraphs have established, our judgment is often faulty and compro-mised, not to say blinded. This is the dilemma of all human ac-tion, but particularly acute for the statesman whose firmness in the face of epistemic uncertainty is maintained for the sake of the whole. Although having earlier quoted the biblical injunc-tion to judge not lest we be judged, Lincoln has not forsworn human judgment. Even as he partially shifts responsibility for the war onto the divinity, he insists, in the final paragraph, on continued human agency.

What is to be done? First, the war—"the work we are in"— still needs winning. At the same time and after, "the nation's wounds" must be tended. Note the very different valence of the word "wounds" in this speech as compared to the Lyceum Ad-dress, which also ended with a reference to "wounds." The scars of those wounds belonged to the veterans of the Revolution then passing from the scene. Since they reminded citizens of the nation's birth, that living history was salutary. The present wounds, in contrast, must be bound up, for they remind citizens of civil strife. The wounds here are intangible—the sectional wounds of the nation's attempted suicide and the psychological wounds of mastery and slavery. Of course, Lincoln does not forget the tangible wounds, calling for care for the veterans and the families of the fallen, perhaps remembering "the maimed, and the widows, and orphans" of 2nd Maccabees 8:28. Care for the vulnerable could become a unifying endeavor. Lincoln's sympathy toward the bereaved is well-known from the letter to Mrs. Bixby. Less known is that Lincoln was in earnest about applying this consideration to all. It was his letter in May 1864 to Senator Charles Sumner, drawing attention to the situation of African American common-law wives, that led directly to legislation equalizing the treatment of war widows. The care to which Lincoln summons the nation at the conclusion of the Second Inaugural emphatically includes Black veterans and their families.

The final action is more general: "to do all which may achieve and cherish" peace, domestically "among ourselves" and internationally "with all nations." Perhaps the most intriguing and surprising word in this clause is "cherish." It is an oddly intimate word. Lincoln might have said "to do all which may achieve and *maintain* . . . peace." "Cherish," though, tells us more than "maintain" or "keep," since it highlights the spirit that leads to that result. Just as the Lyceum Address linked the maintenance or perpetuation of our political institutions to reverence, the idea here is that the maintenance or lastingness of peace depends on holding it dear. The nurturing spirit in which we "do all" matters. "Cherish" also echoes "charity." Significantly, both words are derived from the same Latin root: *carus* (dear). Placed in between "charity" and "cherish" is "care"—although "care" is Germanic rather than Latin in origin (and originally denoted sorrow and grief), the meanings of the three overlap, reinforcing the message of benevolence.

And now, coming full circle, we encounter the stress in the speech's final sentence on the word "all." Three times it is used here, attaining its maximal extension each time. A quick review of its ten occurrences through the speech shows the development. Lincoln started with all Unionists in the first paragraph. In the second paragraph, the reference encompassed the "all" composed of "both parties" to the war. By the end of the third paragraph, the term expanded further to include the slaves and all their stolen labor. Finally, in the universalizing fourth paragraph, Lincoln calls on his listeners to feel "charity for all," to strive "to do all" that accords with peace properly understood, closing with a global extension to "all nations."

The assassination of Abraham Lincoln deprived the American people of the statesman best equipped to follow his own advice. How much difference it would have made is impossible to know. Yet, for us today, the most important thing is that the words and example of Lincoln remain. Through that invention of the written word of which Lincoln thought so highly, he can communicate his thoughts to us and we in turn can converse with him. Though not equal to the omnipresence of the divine, about which Lincoln spoke so beautifully in his Springfield Farewell, Lincoln's speeches "can go with me, and remain with you and be every where for good." His spirit abides. If we listen and reflect, all may yet be well.

APPENDIX: THE TEXTS

The Perpetuation of Our Political Institutions:
Address Before the Young Men's
Lyceum of Springfield, Illinois
January 27, 1838

(1) As a subject for the remarks of the evening, *the perpetuation of our political institutions*, is selected.

(2) In the great journal of things happening under the sun, we, the American People, find our account running, under date of the nineteenth century of the Christian era.—We find ourselves in the peaceful possession, of the fairest portion of the earth, as regards extent of territory, fertility of soil, and salubrity of climate. We find ourselves under the government of a system of political institutions, conducing more essentially to the ends of civil and religious liberty, than any of which the history of former times tells us. We, when mounting the stage of existence, found ourselves the legal inheritors of these fundamental blessings. We toiled not in the acquirement or establishment of them—they are a legacy bequeathed us, by a *once* hardy, brave, and patriotic, but *now* lamented and departed race of ancestors.

Their's was the task (and nobly they performed it) to possess themselves, and through themselves, us, of this goodly land; and to uprear upon its hills and its valleys, a political edifice of liberty and equal rights; 'tis ours only, to transmit these, the former, unprofaned by the foot of an invader; the latter, undecayed by the lapse of time and untorn by usurpation, to the latest generation that fate shall permit the world to know. This task of gratitude to our fathers, justice to ourselves, duty to posterity, and love for our species in general, all imperatively require us faithfully to perform.

(3) How then shall we perform it?—At what point shall we expect the approach of danger? By what means shall we fortify against it?—Shall we expect some transatlantic military giant, to step the Ocean, and crush us at a blow? Never!—All the armies of Europe, Asia and Africa combined, with all the treasure of the earth (our own excepted) in their military chest; with a Buonaparte for a commander, could not by force, take a drink from the Ohio, or make a track on the Blue Ridge, in a trial of a thousand years.

(4) At what point then is the approach of danger to be expected? I answer, if it ever reach us, it must spring up amongst us. It cannot come from abroad. If destruction be our lot, we must ourselves be its author and finisher. As a nation of freemen, we must live through all time, or die by suicide.

(5) I hope I am over wary; but if I am not, there is, even now, something of ill-omen, amongst us. I mean the increasing disregard for law which pervades the country; the growing dispo-

sition to substitute the wild and furious passions, in lieu of the sober judgment of Courts; and the worse than savage mobs, for the executive ministers of justice. This disposition is awfully fearful in any community; and that it now exists in ours, though grating to our feelings to admit, it would be a violation of truth, and an insult to our intelligence, to deny. Accounts of outrages committed by mobs, form the every-day news of the times. They have pervaded the country, from New England to Louisiana;—they are neither peculiar to the eternal snows of the former, nor the burning suns of the latter;—they are not the creature of climate—neither are they confined to the slave-holding, or the non-slave-holding States. Alike, they spring up among the pleasure hunting masters of Southern slaves, and the order loving citizens of the land of steady habits.—Whatever, then, their cause may be, it is common to the whole country.

(6) It would be tedious, as well as useless, to recount the horrors of all of them. Those happening in the State of Mississippi, and at St. Louis, are, perhaps, the most dangerous in example and revolting to humanity. In the Mississippi case, they first commenced by hanging the regular gamblers; a set of men, certainly not following for a livelihood, a very useful, or very honest occupation; but one which, so far from being forbidden by the laws, was actually licensed by an act of the Legislature, passed but a single year before. Next, negroes, suspected of conspiring to raise an insurrection, were caught up and hanged in all parts of the State: then, white men, supposed to be leagued with the negroes; and finally, strangers, from neighboring States, going thither on business, were, in many instances subjected to the same fate. Thus went on this process of hanging, from gamblers

to negroes, from negroes to white citizens, and from these to strangers; till, dead men were seen literally dangling from the boughs of trees upon every road side; and in numbers almost sufficient, to rival the native Spanish moss of the country, as a drapery of the forest.

(7) Turn, then, to that horror-striking scene at St. Louis. A single victim was only sacrificed there. His story is very short; and is, perhaps, the most highly tragic, of anything of its length, that has ever been witnessed in real life. A mulatto man, by the name of McIntosh, was seized in the street, dragged to the suburbs of the city, chained to a tree, and actually burned to death; and all within a single hour from the time he had been a freeman, attending to his own business, and at peace with the world.

(8) Such are the effects of mob law; and such are the scenes, becoming more and more frequent in this land so lately famed for love of law and order; and the stories of which, have even now grown too familiar, to attract any thing more, than an idle remark.

(9) But you are, perhaps, ready to ask, "What has this to do with the perpetuation of our political institutions?" I answer, it has much to do with it. Its direct consequences are, comparatively speaking, but a small evil; and much of its danger consists, in the proneness of our minds, to regard its direct, as its only consequences. Abstractly considered, the hanging of the gamblers at Vicksburg, was of but little consequence. They constitute a portion of population, that is worse than useless in any community; and their death, if no pernicious example be set by it,

is never matter of reasonable regret with any one. If they were annually swept, from the stage of existence, by the plague or small pox, honest men would, perhaps, be much profited, by the operation.—Similar too, is the correct reasoning, in regard to the burning of the negro at St. Louis. He had forfeited his life, by the perpetration of an outrageous murder, upon one of the most worthy and respectable citizens of the city; and had not he died as he did, he must have died by the sentence of the law, in a very short time afterwards. As to him alone, it was as well the way it was, as it could otherwise have been.—But the example in either case, was fearful.—When men take it in their heads to day, to hang gamblers, or burn murderers, they should recollect, that, in the confusion usually attending such transactions, they will be as likely to hang or burn some one who is neither a gambler nor a murderer as one who is; and that, acting upon the example they set, the mob of to-morrow, may, and probably will, hang or burn some of them by the very same mistake. And not only so; the innocent, those who have ever set their faces against violations of law in every shape, alike with the guilty, fall victims to the ravages of mob law; and thus it goes on, step by step, till all the walls erected for the defence of the persons and property of individuals, are trodden down, and disregarded. But all this even, is not the full extent of the evil.—By such examples, by instances of the perpetrators of such acts going unpunished, the lawless in spirit, are encouraged to become lawless in practice; and having been used to no restraint, but dread of punishment, they thus become, absolutely unrestrained.—Having ever regarded Government as their deadliest bane, they make a jubilee of the suspension of its operations; and pray for nothing so much, as its total annihilation. While, on the other hand, good men, men who love tranquility, who desire to abide by the laws, and enjoy their benefits, who would gladly spill their blood in the defence of their country; seeing their property destroyed; their families insulted, and their lives endangered; their persons injured; and seeing nothing in prospect that forebodes a change for the better; become tired of, and disgusted with, a Government that offers them no protection; and are not much averse to a change in which they imagine they have nothing to lose. Thus, then, by the operation of this mobocractic spirit, which all must admit, is now abroad in the land, the strongest bulwark of any Government, and particularly of those constituted like ours, may effectually be broken down and destroyed—I mean the *attachment* of the People. Whenever this effect shall be produced among us; whenever the vicious portion of population shall be permitted to gather in bands of hundreds and thousands, and burn churches, ravage and rob provision-stores, throw printing presses into rivers, shoot editors, and hang and burn obnoxious persons at pleasure, and with impunity; depend on it, this Government cannot last. By such things, the feelings of the best citizens will become more or less alienated from it; and thus it will be left without friends, or with too few, and those few too weak, to make their friendship effectual. At such a time and under such circumstances, men of sufficient talent and ambition will not be wanting to seize the opportunity, strike the blow, and overturn that fair fabric, which for the last half century, has been the fondest hope, of the lovers of freedom, throughout the world.

(10) I know the American People are *much* attached to their Government;—I know they would suffer *much* for its sake;—I know

they would endure evils long and patiently, before they would ever think of exchanging it for another. Yet, notwithstanding all this, if the laws be continually despised and disregarded, if their rights to be secure in their persons and property, are held by no better tenure than the caprice of a mob, the alienation of their affections from the Government is the natural consequence; and to that, sooner or later, it must come.

(11) Here then, is one point at which danger may be expected.

(12) The question recurs, "how shall we fortify against it?" The answer is simple. Let every American, every lover of liberty, every well wisher to his posterity, swear by the blood of the Revolution, never to violate in the least particular, the laws of the country; and never to tolerate their violation by others. As the patriots of seventy-six did to the support of the Declaration of Independence, so to the support of the Constitution and Laws, let every American pledge his life, his property, and his sacred honor;—let every man remember that to violate the law, is to trample on the blood of his father, and to tear the character of his own, and his children's liberty. Let reverence for the laws, be breathed by every American mother, to the lisping babe, that prattles on her lap—let it be taught in schools, in seminaries, and in colleges; let it be written in Primers, spelling books, and in Almanacs;—let it be preached from the pulpit, proclaimed in legislative halls, and enforced in courts of justice. And, in short, let it become the *political religion* of the nation; and let the old and the young, the rich and the poor, the grave and the gay, of all sexes and tongues, and colors and conditions, sacrifice unceasingly upon its altars.

(13) While ever a state of feeling, such as this, shall universally, or even, very generally prevail throughout the nation, vain will be every effort, and fruitless every attempt, to subvert our national freedom.

(14) When I so pressingly urge a strict observance of all the laws, let me not be understood as saying there are no bad laws, nor that grievances may not arise, for the redress of which, no legal provisions have been made.—I mean to say no such thing. But I do mean to say, that, although bad laws, if they exist, should be repealed as soon as possible, still while they continue in force, for the sake of example, they should be religiously observed. So also in unprovided cases. If such arise, let proper legal provisions be made for them with the least possible delay; but, till then, let them, if not too intolerable, be borne with.

(15) There is no grievance that is a fit object of redress by mob law. In any case that arises, as for instance, the promulgation of abolitionism, one of two positions is necessarily true; that is, the thing is right within itself, and therefore deserves the protection of all law and all good citizens; or, it is wrong, and therefore proper to be prohibited by legal enactments; and in neither case, is the interposition of mob law, either necessary, justifiable, or excusable.

(16) But, it may be asked, why suppose danger to our political institutions? Have we not preserved them for more than fifty years? And why may we not for fifty times as long?

(17) We hope there is *no sufficient* reason. We hope all dangers may be overcome; but to conclude that no danger may ever arise,

would itself be extremely dangerous. There are now, and will hereafter be, many causes, dangerous in their tendency, which have not existed heretofore; and which are not too insignificant to merit attention. That our government should have been maintained in its original form from its establishment until now, is not much to be wondered at. It had many props to support it through that period, which now are decayed, and crumbled away. Through that period, it was felt by all, to be an undecided experiment; now, it is understood to be a successful one.—Then, all that sought celebrity and fame, and distinction, expected to find them in the success of that experiment. Their *all* was staked upon it:— their destiny was *inseparably* linked with it. Their ambition aspired to display before an admiring world, a practical demonstration of the truth of a proposition, which had hitherto been considered, at best no better, than problematical; namely, *the capability of a people to govern themselves.* If they succeeded, they were to be immortalized; their names were to be transferred to counties and cities, and rivers and mountains; and to be revered and sung, and toasted through all time. If they failed, they were to be called knaves and fools, and fanatics for a fleeting hour; then to sink and be forgotten. They succeeded. The experiment is successful; and thousands have won their deathless names in making it so. But the game is caught; and I believe it is true, that with the catching, end the pleasures of the chase. This field of glory is harvested, and the crop is already appropriated. But new reapers will arise, and *they*, too, will seek a field. It is to deny, what the history of the world tells us is true, to suppose that men of ambition and talents will not continue to spring up amongst us. And, when they do, they will as naturally seek the gratification of their ruling passion, as others have so done before them. The question then, is, can that gratification be found in supporting and maintaining an edifice that has been erected by others? Most certainly it cannot. Many great and good men sufficiently qualified for any task they should undertake, may ever be found, whose ambition would inspire to nothing beyond a seat in Congress, a gubernatorial or a presidential chair; *but such belong not to the family of the lion, or the tribe of the eagle.* What! think you these places would satisfy an Alexander, a Caesar, or a Napoleon?—Never! Towering genius disdains a beaten path. It seeks regions hitherto unexplored.—It sees *no distinction* in adding story to story, upon the monuments of fame, erected to the memory of others. It *denies* that it is glory enough to serve under any chief. It *scorns* to tread in the footsteps of *any* predecessor, however illustrious. It thirsts and burns for distinction; and, if possible, it will have it, whether at the expense of emancipating slaves, or enslaving freemen. Is it unreasonable then to expect, that some man possessed of the loftiest genius, coupled with ambition sufficient to push it to its utmost stretch, will at some time, spring up among us? And when such a one does, it will require the people to be united with each other, attached to the government and laws, and generally intelligent, to successfully frustrate his designs.

(18) Distinction will be his paramount object, and although he would as willingly, perhaps more so, acquire it by doing good as harm; yet, that opportunity being past, and nothing left to be done in the way of building up, he would set boldly to the task of pulling down.

(19) Here, then, is a probable case, highly dangerous, and such a one as could not have well existed heretofore.

(20) Another reason which *once was*; but which, to the same extent, is *now no more*, has done much in maintaining our institutions thus far. I mean the powerful influence which the interesting scenes of the revolution had upon the *passions* of the people as distinguished from their judgment. By this influence, the jealousy, envy, and avarice, incident to our nature, and so common to a state of peace, prosperity, and conscious strength, were, for the time, in a great measure smothered and rendered inactive; while the deep-rooted principles of *hate*, and the powerful motive of *revenge*, instead of being turned against each other, were directed exclusively against the British nation. And thus, from the force of circumstances, the basest principles of our nature, were either made to lie dormant, or to become the active agents in the advancement of the noblest of cause—that of establishing and maintaining civil and religious liberty.

(21) But this state of feeling *must fade, is fading, has faded*, with the circumstances that produced it.

(22) I do not mean to say, that the scenes of the revolution *are now* or *ever will* be entirely forgotten; but that like every thing else, they must fade upon the memory of the world, and grow more and more dim by the lapse of time. In history, we hope, they will be read of, and recounted, so long as the bible shall be read;—but even granting that they will, their influence *cannot be* what it heretofore has been. Even then, they *cannot be* so universally known, nor so vividly felt, as they were by the generation just gone to rest. At the close of that struggle, nearly every adult male had been a participator in some of its scenes. The

consequence was, that of those scenes, in the form of a husband, a father, a son or a brother, *a living history* was to be found in every family—a history bearing the indubitable testimonies of its own authenticity, in the limbs mangled, in the scars of wounds received, in the midst of the very scenes related—a history, too, that could be read and understood alike by all, the wise and the ignorant, the learned and the unlearned.—But *those* histories are gone. They *can* be read no more forever. They *were* a fortress of strength; but, what invading foeman could *never do*, the silent artillery of time *has done*; the leveling of its walls. They are gone.—They *were* a forest of giant oaks; but the all-resistless hurricane has swept over them, and left only, here and there, a lonely trunk, despoiled of its verdure, shorn of its foliage; unshading and unshaded, to murmur in a few gentle breezes, and to combat with its mutilated limbs, a few more ruder storms, then to sink, and be no more.

(23) They *were* the pillars of the temple of liberty; and now, that they have crumbled away, that temple must fall, unless we, their descendants, supply their places with other pillars, hewn from the solid quarry of sober reason. Passion has helped us; but can do so no more. It will in future be our enemy. Reason, cold, calculating, unimpassioned reason, must furnish all the materials for our future support and defence.—Let those materials be moulded into *general intelligence, sound morality*, and in particular, *a reverence for the constitution and laws*: and, that we improved to the last; that we remained free to the last; that we revered his name to the last; that, during his long sleep, we permitted no hostile foot to pass over or desecrate his resting

place; shall be that which to learn the last trump shall awaken our WASHINGTON.

(24) Upon these let the proud fabric of freedom rest, as the rock of its basis; and as truly as has been said of the only greater institution, *"the gates of hell shall not prevail against it."*

Address Delivered at the Dedication of
the Cemetery at Gettysburg
November 19, 1863

Four score and seven years ago our fathers brought forth on this continent, a new nation, conceived in Liberty, and dedicated to the proposition that all men are created equal.

Now we are engaged in a great civil war, testing whether that nation, or any nation so conceived and so dedicated, can long endure. We are met on a great battle-field of that war. We have come to dedicate a portion of that field, as a final resting place for those who here gave their lives that that nation might live. It is altogether fitting and proper that we should do this.

But, in a larger sense, we can not dedicate—we can not consecrate—we can not hallow—this ground. The brave men, living and dead, who struggled here, have consecrated it, far above our poor power to add or detract. The world will little note, nor long remember what we say here, but it can never forget what they did here. It is for us the living, rather, to be dedicated here to the unfinished work which they who fought here have thus far so nobly advanced. It is rather for us to be here dedicated to the great task remaining before us—that from these honored dead we take increased devotion to that cause for which they gave the last full measure of devotion—that we here highly resolve that these dead shall not have died in vain—that this nation, under God, shall have a new birth of freedom—and that government of the people, by the people, for the people, shall not perish from the earth.

Second Inaugural Address
March 4, 1865

Fellow Countrymen:

At this second appearing to take the oath of the presidential office, there is less occasion for an extended address than there was at the first. Then a statement, somewhat in detail, of a course to be pursued, seemed fitting and proper. Now, at the expiration of four years, during which public declarations have been constantly called forth on every point and phase of the great contest which still absorbs the attention, and engrosses the energies of the nation, little that is new could be presented. The progress of our arms, upon which all else chiefly depends, is as well known to the public as to myself; and it is, I trust, reasonably satisfactory and encouraging to all. With high hope for the future, no prediction in regard to it is ventured.

On the occasion corresponding to this four years ago, all thoughts were anxiously directed to an impending civil-war. All dreaded it—all sought to avert it. While the inaugeral address was being delivered from this place, devoted altogether to *saving* the Union without war, insurgent agents were in the city seeking to *destroy* it without war—seeking to dissolve the Union, and divide effects, by negotiation. Both parties deprecated war; but one of them would *make* war rather than let the nation survive; and the other would *accept* war rather than let it perish. And the war came.

One eighth of the whole population were colored slaves, not distributed generally over the Union, but localized in the Southern part of it. These slaves constituted a peculiar and powerful interest. All knew that this interest was, somehow, the cause of the war. To strengthen, perpetuate, and extend this interest was the object for which the insurgents would rend the Union, even by war; while the government claimed no right to do more than to restrict the territorial enlargement of it. Neither party expected for the war, the magnitude, or the duration, which it has already attained. Neither anticipated that the *cause* of the conflict might cease with, or even before, the conflict itself should cease. Each looked for an easier triumph, and a result less fundamental and astounding. Both read the same Bible, and pray to the same God; and each invokes His aid against the other. It may seem strange that any men should dare to ask a just God's assistance in wringing their bread from the sweat of other men's faces; but let us judge not that we be not judged. The prayers of both could not be answered; that of neither has been answered fully. The Almighty has His own purposes. "Woe unto the world because of offences! for it must needs be that offences come; but woe to that man by whom the offence cometh!" If we shall suppose that American Slavery is one of those offences which, in the providence of God, must needs come, but which, having continued through His appointed time, He now wills to remove, and that He gives to both North and South, this terrible war, as the woe due to those by whom the offence came, shall we discern therein any departure from those divine attributes which the believers in a Living God always ascribe to Him? Fondly do we hope—fervently do we pray—that this mighty scourge of war may speedily pass away. Yet, if God wills that it continue, until all the wealth piled by the bond-man's two hundred and fifty years of unrequited toil shall be sunk, and until every drop of blood drawn with the lash, shall be paid by another drawn with the sword, as was said three thousand years ago, so still it must be said "the judgments of the Lord, are true and righteous altogether."

With malice toward none; with charity for all; with firmness in the right, as God gives us to see the right, let us strive on to finish the work we are in; to bind up the nation's wounds; to care for him who shall have borne the battle, and for his widow, and his orphan—to do all which may achieve and cherish a just, and a lasting peace, among ourselves, and with all nations.

ACKNOWLEDGEMENTS

〜

There is no one who walked the earth, with the sole exception of Jesus, who is more written about than Abraham Lincoln. Although much of this scholarship is excellent, I have tried to take a more independent path, working directly from Lincoln's words as I encourage my students to do. Frederick Douglass, in his great oration on Lincoln, testified that "The image of the man went out with his words, and those who read him knew him." Trusting that to be true, I have gone light on footnoting other scholars. That choice, however, means that my debt to other and better students of Lincoln needs to be acknowledged, albeit inadequately, here.

My primary debt is to Harry Jaffa, whose pioneering book *The Crisis of the House Divided* claimed Lincoln for political philosophy. My short list of other classic guides includes Jacques

Barzun, Lord Charnwood, William Lee Miller, and Richard Weaver, and among living Lincolnians, Eva Brann, John Channing Briggs, Allen Guelzo, Lewis Lehrman, Lucas Morel, Greg Weiner, and Michael Zuckert. I was blessed to have as readers of the manuscript two of my long-ago teachers from the University of Chicago, Leon Kass and Ralph Lerner, both of whom have written insightfully and beautifully on Lincoln. My deeply learned and dear friend Paul Seaton was kind enough to keep after me about my progress and then to read and critique each installment. I am indebted to two outstanding scholars and friends, Pete Myers and Peter Ahrensdorf, for some very challenging and helpful remarks (to which I have insufficiently responded, I fear) about the last chapter.

Over the years, colleagues at other institutions have generously asked me to give Lincoln-themed public lectures, and I have benefited immensely from those engagements, including the dinner discussions and subsequent email exchanges. I owe special thanks to Robby George and Brad Wilson at the James Madison Program for their invitation to deliver the Charles E. Test Distinguished Lecture Series at Princeton in 2019. Those lectures allowed me to develop my understanding of Lincoln as a statesman of racial reconciliation. An earlier version of the Gettysburg Address chapter appeared in *National Affairs* in spring 2014. I am beholden to the journal's distinguished editor, Yuval Levin, for permission to republish it. Even more, I appreciate his offer to join the Social, Cultural, and Constitutional Studies program at the American Enterprise Institute. AEI's support included the super-competent research services of Jackson Wolford.

I owe special thanks to Bill Kristol and Andy Zwick for convincing me to participate in a couple of Kristol's stimulating *Conversations*. It was the Lincoln podcast that led Stephen Power, formerly executive editor at Thomas Dunne Books, to propose the idea for this book. Stephen's initial encouragement and guidance were invaluable. Kevin Reilly, Alan Bradshaw, and the top-notch team at St. Martin's Press saw the book through its stages with impeccable professional skill. The writing never would have been completed if not for course releases from my teaching responsibilities made possible by the generous patronage of Tom Klingenstein, who believes unwaveringly in Lincoln's America.

Although I needed a break from teaching to finish the book, the classroom has always been the most energizing place for me to be. It has been a privilege to pore over Lincoln's works with undergraduates at my home institution of Loyola University Maryland, as well as students at Princeton, Harvard, and the Hertog Political Studies Program—heartfelt thanks to Robby George, Harvey Mansfield, Roger Hertog, and Cheryl Miller for making those teaching stints possible. My interpretations of the texts have emerged from the questions raised and discoveries made during Lincoln seminars. These terrific students, in their openness to serious reading and reflection, have always sustained my hope in the American future.

Writing a book, even a short one, is demanding. At my side throughout has been Lauren Weiner, partner for forty wonderful years, wife for six. Lauren's confidence in the project buoyed me up and her own impressive skills as a writer and editor greatly improved the manuscript. No one else read it with quite the same sharp eye for error, nuanced feel for language, and sensitivity to authorial aims. To our son, Jameer: as the ideal reader I had in mind all along, I hope you like it. It's your summer reading assignment.

NOTES

CHAPTER 1: THE LYCEUM ADDRESS

1. Abraham Lincoln, Lyceum Address, https://www.youtube.com /watch?v=GBrPqD1Mnw.

2. Daniel Webster, "Address at the Laying of the Cornerstone of the Bunker Hill Monument," in *American Speeches: Political Oratory from the Revolution to the Civil War* (New York: Literary Classics of the United States, Inc., 2006), 124.

3. Henry Wilson, *History of the Rise and Fall of the Slave Power in America*, vol. 2 (Boston: James R. Osgood and Company, 1874), 660.

4. The phrase "perpetual and national" appears in Lincoln's Speech in Reply to Douglas at Springfield, Illinois on July 17, 1858, and again in the second and fifth debates with Douglas.

5. It may be because of the actual heightened danger of sectionalism that Lincoln is careful to draw attention away from the sectional complexion of this alienation.

6. For examples, see John Channing Briggs, "Steeped in Shakespeare," *Claremont Review of Books*, vol. 9, no. 1 (winter 2008/09).

7. I use "rhetoric" in its classical meaning, distinguishing between persuasion directed at the truth and sophistry (think "spin," "hype," "false facts," and all the other deceptions). Of course, because many of the techniques of persuasion are shared between the rhetor and the sophist, telling them apart is not easy. To my ears, Stephen Douglas was a sophist, Lincoln a rhetor—a good person speaking well for the common good. Those who voted for Douglas didn't perceive it that way.

8. The distribution of the questions in paragraphs 3, 4, 9, 12, 16, and 17 helps to mark the sections of the speech. There are four questions in paragraph 3, with the last followed by the single word "Never!" There is one question in paragraph 4, followed by the phrase "I answer. . . ." There is one question in paragraph 9, followed by the phrase "I answer. . . ." There is one question in paragraph 12, followed by the sentence "The answer is simple." There are three questions in paragraph 16, followed by the phrase "We hope. . . ." There are three questions in paragraph 17, one of them followed by the single word "Never!" Both of the "Never!" exclamations are linked to mentions of Napoleon.

9. This is a remarkable document worthy of careful study, especially since in his 1860 campaign biography, Lincoln included the full text of the 1837 Protest, asserting that it "briefly defined his position on the slavery question; and so far as it goes, it was then the same that it is now." The document begins by re-centering the debate on the wrongfulness of slavery, while agreeing that extremist abolitionist rhetoric is divisive. Then, by drawing attention to the differences between the Illinois resolutions and the U.S. Constitution, he sets forth his understanding of both the limits and the available powers of the federal authority with respect to slavery. With terse precision, he corrects the misconstructions of the Constitution that were beginning to take hold, such as the difference between stating that there is a "sacred right" to hold slaves "under the Constitution" (the false wording of the Illinois resolutions) and stating that there is no federal power to interfere with the pre-existing institution within the slave states.

10. Clement Eaton, "Mob Violence in the Old South," *The Mississippi Valley Historical Review*, vol. 29, no. 3 (December 1942): 351–70.

11. Lincoln will make this same move in the Peoria Address, where his thesis is that the 1854 Kansas-Nebraska Act is "wrong in its direct effect . . . and wrong in its prospective principle." There, too, it is the long-term consequences that are most consequential.

12. His strategy might be seen as similar to the rhetorical path taken by Diodotus in his debate with the demagogue Cleon in Thucydides (*The Peloponnesian War* 3.36–50). Also, see chapter 7 of Clifford Orwin, *The Humanity of Thucydides* (Princeton, NJ: Princeton University Press, 1994), 142–62.

13. New Testament passages that deliver this counsel include 1st Corinthians 7:21–24; Ephesians 6:5–8; Colossians 3:22–24; and 1st Peter 2:18–25.

14. Martin Luther King, Jr., "Letter from a Birmingham Jail," in *I Have a Dream: Writings and Speeches that Changed the World*, ed. James Melvin Washington (Glenview, IL: Scott, Foresman and Company, 1992), 90.

15. Malcolm X, "A Declaration of Independence" and "The Ballot or the Bullet," in *Malcolm X Speaks: Selected Speeches and Statements*, ed. George Breitman (New York: Grove Weidenfeld, 1990), 22, 32, 33–34, 44.

16. Lincoln was aware of this problem. In the First Inaugural, at the same time that he indicates his intention to enforce the law, he suggests it is in need of correction: "in any law upon this subject, ought not all the safeguards of liberty known in civilized and humane jurisprudence to be introduced, so that a free man be not, in any case, surrendered as a slave?" Although the speech is often read as conciliatory toward the South, in fact, elements of Lincoln's constitutionalism are anything but conciliatory. For instance, he recommends enforcement of the "privileges and immunities" clause, which would have challenged southern efforts to deprive abolitionists, free Blacks, and Republicans of constitutional rights.

17. While some Union troops were killed in battle, a large number (Black soldiers in particular) were massacred after surrendering. This is without question one of the most disgraceful episodes of the war. The Confederate general in command was Nathan Bedford Forrest, notorious after the war as the first Grand Wizard of the Ku Klux Klan.

18. In 1848, during his only term in the U.S. House of Representatives, Lincoln put forward a proposal (unsuccessful) for the abolition of slavery in the District. Its carefully composed features provide

a good window into Lincoln's brand of anti-slavery action. Along with elements often present in gradual emancipation statutes, it contained a unique requirement: a mandate that those to be freed receive education in advance.

19. Michael Burlingame convincingly shows the similarity of language between this passage and the satirical attack upon Stephen Douglas that appeared in the *Sangamo Journal* on the day of Lincoln's lecture. The "Conservative" series, purportedly written by a disgruntled Democratic critic, seems to have been the work of Lincoln himself. Lincoln's audience might well have picked up on the coded reference to the "towering genius" (a bit of raillery at the expense of the 5'4" Douglas from the 6'4" Lincoln) for whom "a seat in Congress is not worthy to be your abiding place." See Michael Burlingame, *Abraham Lincoln: A Life* (Baltimore, MD: The Johns Hopkins University Press, 2008), vol. 1, 139–41 and *Sangamo Journal*, January 27, 1838, available at https://idnc.library.illinois.edu/?a=d&d

20. See Diana Schaub, "Abraham Lincoln and the Spirit of Invention" in *The New Atlantis* (fall 2021).

CHAPTER 2: THE GETTYSBURG ADDRESS

1. Lincoln, a baseball fan, might have been familiar with another form of scorecard, the recent invention of the box score in 1859.

2. This was not just a *pro forma* statement. Surveying Republican platforms in the nineteenth century, only those of 1856, 1860, 1868, and 1876 reference the Declaration. There is then a one hundred–year gap until the platform of 1976 mentions it (in a call to celebrate the nation's bicentennial). There are echoes of the Declaration in 1932 on the rights of Black Americans and in 1956 on rights from the Creator. The platform of 1996 concludes with an explicit reaffirmation of the truths of the Declaration. Beginning in 2000, the Republican platform has invoked the Declaration in the context of a call for a right-to-life amendment.

On the other side, Democratic platforms from 1840 to 1856 mention the Declaration but only in the context of immigration policy.

(The Declaration is mentioned again in 1884, but with a shift against immigration.) Neither of the two platforms adopted by the splintered Democrats in 1860 makes any mention of the Declaration. After that, the Democratic platforms of 1900 and 1976 reaffirm the truths of the Declaration. The others make no explicit mention of the document, although there are echoes of its language in 1956 and 1960 through references to equal rights and the rights of man. Additionally, the Democrats frequently invoke the name of the Declaration's primary author, Thomas Jefferson, and the Republicans do the same for its greatest defender, Abraham Lincoln.

3. Briggs refers his readers to Eva Brann's marvelous 1976 essay, "A Reading of the Gettysburg Address," in *Abraham Lincoln, the Gettysburg Address, and American Constitutionalism*, ed. Leo Paul S. Alvarez (Dallas: University of Dallas Press, 1976), 21–52.

4. In his eulogy of Henry Clay, Lincoln takes the same anti-ceremonial stance. He notes of Clay that "All his efforts were made for practical effect. He never spoke merely to be heard. He never delivered a Fourth of July oration, or a eulogy on an occasion like this." With wonderful adeptness, Lincoln outdoes Clay by transforming a eulogy of Clay into a speech with practical effect. Lincoln binds the memory of Clay to the antislavery cause, thereby attempting to forestall leading Democrats (especially Stephen Douglas) from misappropriating Clay's reputation for the purpose of compromise-oriented pandering to the slaveocrats.

5. During the past three decades, preposition use by students in their speech and writing has become more imprecise—the relations between substantives elude them. Emblematic is their confusion about their own relation to their alma maters. They speak of "graduating high school" or "graduating college" which is a logical impossibility since it is the institution of learning that does the graduating. It determines whether the candidate for graduation is meritorious and it awards the degree. Unfortunately, the proper transitive use of "to graduate" has pretty much disappeared. When used instead as an intransitive verb, "to graduate" requires a preposition: He graduated from Lincoln High.

NOTES

CHAPTER 3: THE SECOND INAUGURAL

1. In the King James Bible, there are six verses that speak of His appearing: 1st Timothy 6:14, 2nd Timothy 1:10, 2nd Timothy 4:1, 2nd Timothy 4:8, Titus 2:13, and 1st Peter 1:7.

2. The only other inaugural address that avoids "I" with the same thoroughness is Franklin Delano Roosevelt's 1941 Third Inaugural. He has a similarly positioned "I hope" mirroring Lincoln's "I trust."

3. The phrase is from his last public address (on April 11, 1865), in which he did begin to lay out a program for "restoring the proper practical relations between these States and the Union."

4. Editors often indicate the misspelling. My hunch is that it was deliberately nonstandard. Lincoln does occasionally write in dialect, as when he complained of Stephen Douglas toward the close of the House Divided speech: "How can he oppose the advances of slavery? He don't *care* anything about it. His avowed *mission is impressing* the 'public heart' to *care* nothing about it."

5. I don't mean to overlook the large numbers of Blacks who fought for freedom through the Union, but that became possible only after the issuance of Lincoln's Emancipation Proclamation.

6. By contrast, the first Bible references to "body" are to "dead body" and the regulations regarding uncleanness. The matter of the body becomes more complicated in the New Testament through the body of Christ.

7. Jamestown was an English settlement, but there were slaves introduced into North America even earlier by other colonial powers. Lincoln was aware of the wider context as he showed in his Lecture on Discoveries and Inventions, where he offered another date, 1434, for the beginning of transatlantic slavery. Using the mordantly scathing phrase, "the invention of negroes, or, of the present mode of using them," Lincoln indicates that the tremendous technological advances of the age of exploration also gave rise to the morally retrograde idea that other human beings could be branded, packaged, and shipped as commodities.

INDEX